Educating for a Change

Rick Arnold
Bev Burke
Carl James
D'Arcy Martin
Barb Thomas

Doris Marshall Institute for Education and Action

between the lines

Co-published by Between the Lines,
720 Bathurst Street, #404, Toronto, Ontario M5S 2R4 Canada

and

Doris Marshall Institute for Education and Action,

Design and illustration by Margie Bruun-Meyer / Art Work
Typeset by Coach House Printing, Toronto
Printed in Canada

"Why We Sing" by Mario Benedetti was translated by D'Arcy Martin. Every attempt has been made to secure permission to reprint the poems "Why We Sing" by Mario Benedetti from *Inventario – Poesia Completa (1950-1981)* published by Visor Libros, Spain, and "You who think I find words for everything" by Adrienne Rich from *Your Native Land, Your Life: Poems* published by W.W. Norton and Co. (Inc.) U.S.A.

Between the Lines receives financial assistance from the Canada Council, the Ontario Arts Council, and the Department of Communications.

The Doris Marshall Institute for Education and Action received project funding assistance in writing this book from the Ontario Ministry of Education.

Reprinted: September 2005

Canadian Cataloguing in Publication Data

Main entry under title:

Educating for a change

Includes bibliographical references.
ISBN 0-921284-47-0 (bound)   ISBN 0-921284-48-9 (pbk.)

1. Community education.   2. Democracy.   3. Education – Aims and objectives.   I. Arnold, Rick, 1948-

LC1036.E38 1991   370.19'4   C91-093611-0

To
Fran Endicott, dian marino and Herbet de Souza
educators of humour, courage, skill, and commitment.

Why We Sing

If each hour brings its death
if time is a den of thieves
the breezes carry a scent of evil
and life is just a moving target

you will ask why we sing

if our finest people are shunned
our homeland is dying of sorrow
and the human heart is shattered
even before shame explodes

you will ask why we sing

if the trees and the sky remain
as far off as the horizon
some absence hovers over the evening
and disappointment colours the morning

you will ask why we sing

we sing because the river is humming
and when the river hums / the river hums
we sing because cruelty has no name
but we can name its destiny
we sing because the child because everything
because in the future because the people
we sing because the survivors
and our dead want us to sing

we sing because shouting is not enough
nor is sorrow or anger
we sing because we believe in people
and we shall overcome these defeats

we sing because the sun recognizes us
and the fields smell of spring
and because in this stem and that fruit
every question has its answer

we sing because it is raining on the furrow
and we are the militants of life
and because we cannot and will not
allow our song to become ashes.

Mario Benedetti
"Por Que Cantamos," Uruguay, 1979

Contents

2

1

3

4

5

6

Introduction

This is a book for all educators – and anyone else interested in how education works – who agree that the time for fuzzy platitudes and top-down practices is over.

How often in the past few years have we heard educational "commandments" like "Respect the people you teach" or "Empower people through learning"? On the surface there's nothing wrong with these statements – they may seem everything we should strive for – except for one very important fact: in the hands of many educational practitioners such concepts work only to fudge the key matter of power.

When you stop to think about it, why should teachers have to be reminded "to respect" their students? Shouldn't this be a given? Why would learners have to be "empowered through learning"? Don't they have power already? These may appear to be elementary questions, but in much education today it seems that taking a position on power is avoided.

In *Educating for a Change* the issue of power is central. Running through the book are two important threads. The first is that education must empower all people to act for change. The second is that this education must be based on a democratic practice: by which we mean creating the conditions for full and equal participation in discussion, debate, and decision-making.

In the following pages we explore the political dimension of learning, and the learning dimension of politics. We hope that this book will help unmask – and not cover up – the power relations in our society.

In taking this stance we assume some shared social and political values with those of you who are reading from the vantage point of educators / activists challenging the status quo. As authors we are writing in Southern Ontario at the start of the 1990s, having like most people suffered through a lean and mean decade under the spell of Reaganomics and Thatcherism. These politicians may be gone but they've left their heavy mark on countries such as Canada, where business and political leaders continue to push a similar line while claiming things are now kinder and gentler.

The book emerges from a process, a set of requests, and a political responsibility. The process is the many meetings and workshops we have conducted over the years, each time promising ourselves and one another that one day our sketchy notes from the event would be drawn together in book form. The requests have been largely from participants in our workshops, who wanted us to demystify the steps in our own work. The political responsibility is to those colleagues and mentors who have helped us along the road, and who now can take back in organized form some of what they have given.

This book aims to build skills and confidence. It is our way of surviving and growing in influence against the grain of individualistic and conservative practices in education and politics. We offer it as a tool in the hands of those with whom we share a vision of transformed power relations – in our own lives and in the outside world.

1

So what's in Educating for a Change?

✦ Chapter one is about strategy: factors to consider before getting involved in an educational program. We discuss the importance of putting ourselves as educators into the picture – and the importance of analysing the broader social context in which our work takes place.

✦ Chapter two draws from our experience in designing educational events so they meet the objectives people bring to them.

✦ Chapter three focuses on educational activities with examples of some we have found useful in the past.

✦ Chapter four is about facing the challenges of facilitating a group, making the most of who we are and working through conflicting agendas.

✦ Chapter five looks back at some of the things we have learned from our past experiences.

✦ Chapter six looks forward to some of the challenges that we believe await us in the 1990s.

✦ The Postscript includes two conversations that would be quite out of place in a more formal, technical manual. The first is from a discussion that the five of us had as we neared the end of the writing process. The second is made up of comments from colleagues who read the manuscript along the way.

In doing the writing we've been constantly reminded of the clutch in the stomach: that moment when we first face a group of participants, in a workshop or a meeting, and wonder how we got into this and how we can possibly get through it. Moments of panic, of doubt and self-doubt, are a recurring nightmare for committed educators. But it is our belief that when we are properly prepared, and clear in our goals, those moments have the potential to generate our richest learning.

We hope that our experience, with its limits and particularities, will strengthen a network of educators engaged in social movements, in Canada and internationally, both inside and outside the formal education structures, in classrooms and in workshops.

We hope that this book, though firmly rooted in a Canadian context, will also be of value to a growing international network of people seeking social justice. Our experience has shown that the methodologies and practices we outline here have wide applicability. For instance, in an African National Congress workshop some of us did in Zambia, many of the participants took the work we did on how to design a workshop and applied it to meetings they were preparing on a variety of policy issues. In fact, we've found that social activists can use the educational approaches in this book for many different collective activities – research, evaluation, policy formulation – as well as for workshops and courses.

We know that learning is often worthwhile just for its own sake. To satisfy individual curiosity, to develop personal capacities, to explore varied and surprising experience: these are expressions of our freedom, our full humanity. In these learnings, comprehensive social strategy is not a central concern.

But education for social change is engaged politically. This is praxis, or theory in action. Those of us engaged in this praxis, whether in community groups, educational institutions, or broad-based social movements, must reflect daily on strategy. Our educational work must be located not so we can shape the grand sweep of history, but so we can exercise our right and obligation to an educated guess about the social impact of the learning we promote.

THE WRITERS   This book is an inside job. The five of us have worked, separately and together, in critical education for social change throughout the 1980s. So writing this book has provided an opportunity to look back on what we have learned and to compare notes on what lies ahead for the 1990s.

The text is written in the first-person plural. All five of us have written other publications, we all have one or more postgraduate academic degrees, and we all are now based in southern Ontario. Yet each of us has brought diverse social identities, views, and habits into our work together.

✦ Bev Burke, who co-ordinated the writing of this book, was born in Ontario and taught secondary school in Canada and Tanzania. She worked in development education at the Cross-Cultural Learner Centre in London, Ontario, with CUSO, and with the Canadian Council for International Co-operation (CCIC). After working for three years in Central America, she has remained engaged in solidarity work through the Latin American Working Group.

✦ Rick Arnold was born in Caracas and educated formally in Venezuela, Canada, and the United States. He was a founding member of the Cross Cultural Communication Centre in Toronto and was later on the staff of the Development Education Centre, also in Toronto. After working with Bev Burke in Central America he led several tours, particularly of Canadian trade unionists, to that region. He participates in the public education work of Tools for Peace and the Latin American Working Group.

✦ Carl James was born in the Caribbean and did post-secondary education in Toronto. Active in community work, he has a special interest in youth issues and anti-racist education. He has taught at a number of post-secondary institutions in Toronto, including York University and Ryerson Polytechnical Institute. He teaches at Sheridan College, where he also co-ordinates an international development project that takes him to Tanzania each year.

✦ D'Arcy Martin was born in Hamilton, Ontario, and studied at the University of Toronto. He was a founding member of the Development Education Centre in Toronto and has participated in international work through the International Council for Adult Education. He has worked in trade union education for over a decade, first with the Steelworkers and then with the Communications and Electrical Workers.

3

✦ Barb Thomas was born in England, grew up in Ottawa, and studied in Kingston and Toronto. She worked for a decade as program co-ordinator of the Cross Cultural Communication Centre and was a founding member of the Centre for Caribbean Dialogue in Toronto. She has worked as an anti-racist educator, writer, and facilitator with boards of education, trade unions, and community organizations. Her primary work now is in educational leadership development.

Because this book is a reflection of our experience, some of the patterns in that experience should be clear from these brief biographies. Broadly, Bev and Rick have worked mostly with international solidarity groups, Barb and Carl with anti-racist educators, and D'Arcy with the trade union movement.

Since 1986 we have all been engaged in the work of the Doris Marshall Institute. Rick, Bev, and Barb work as full-time staff with the DMI, while Carl and D'Arcy are employed elsewhere and volunteer as part of the core group.

Each of us took primary responsibility for a section of the book, which means there is a variety of styles and perspectives in the writing. Yet the process we've followed – collective suggestions, exchange, and feedback – means that each of us is present in all chapters.

The DMI is named for Doris Marshall, a Canadian pioneer of adult education for justice who lives in Toronto. Her convictions about women's rights, international solidarity, and the creative strength of senior adults have influenced her family, her community, and the Institute team. We provide training and skill development in the following areas:

✧ popular education theory and methodology
✧ solidarity education
✧ anti-racist education
✧ facilitator training
✧ participatory research and evaluation
✧ materials production
✧ media analysis and production
✧ network and organization building
✧ process consultation

We try to select our projects based on their potential for building and supporting a broad-based popular movement for social justice in Canada. We have experience in working with – and a strategic commitment to continuing working with – certain constituencies:

✧ international development and solidarity organizations
✧ trade unions
✧ grassroots organizations and community groups
✧ social service workers
✧ cross-sector coalitions

Writing this book, though, highlighted the gaps in our experience. There is little

4

discussion here of work in the churches or of the variety of religious social action organizations. We have only limited direct involvement with the environmental movement, our understanding of Canadian issues and experiences outside southern Ontario is uneven, and our age range from the mid-thirties to mid-forties implies some biases.

We're working from what we know, trying to learn more about what we don't know, and using this book as a vehicle for dialogue with others whose experience and insights will be different from our own. In particular, we have drawn on four workshops conducted in the late 1980s, after we began working together as a team. One workshop was with Education Wife Assault, the second with immigrant community service organizations, the third with anti-racist activists in the Ontario Public Service Employees Union, and the fourth in Southern Africa with the African National Congress.

In the end we have chosen not to "iron out" the different tones and voices of our writing into an authoritative, uniform style. And we haven't "filled in" the gaps – those places where the dynamics are better understood by others – with second-hand experience. We hope that the personal diversity of our writing, and its anchor in our practice, will encourage other educators for social change to reflect, personally and in print, on experiences different from our own, and to develop the appropriate tools and perspectives.

A WORD ABOUT WORDS

This is not a neutral review of meanings.... [It is] a vocabulary to use, to find our own ways in, to change as we find it necessary to change it, as we go on making our own language and history.
– *Raymond Williams*, Keywords: A Vocabulary of Culture and Society

For us, it's important how things get named. So we're going to start by explaining why we've chosen to use certain words and terms. This is not to say that ours are the "correct" definitions – or the only ones. Rather, this is how we've used certain words in this book.

Words about education

Education for social change is the term we use to describe our work in general. It signifies an approach to education that is in the interests of oppressed groups. We involve people in a process of critical analysis so they can, potentially, act collectively to change oppressive structures. The process is participatory, creative, and empowering. The term popular education, a translation of the Spanish *educación popular*, covers this same approach; those of us influenced by Latin American educators use the terms interchangeably.

Educational event is the term we use to describe a structured time for learning, and it includes what happens before, during, and after the event. The term covers words used in both formal and informal settings to describe our work: courses, seminars, conferences, workshops, and meetings. At the Doris

Marshall Institute we also use the word skillshop to describe a workshop where participants develop skills to do social change education.

Educational leadership development describes the structured opportunities in which educators develop the skills to do social change education. Although we like to avoid the word training because it suggests a mechanical, hierarchical transfer of knowledge, we still find it necessary to use the term in certain contexts (in training for trainers, for example).

Popular educator: some of us use this term to describe our role in linking education and organizing. Other words used in this respect are activist educator, community educator/organizer, and social activist.

Facilitation is the word we use to describe our role, on our feet, in an education session. But it's only one among many used for this purpose. Others are course leader, co-ordinator, and animator. We tend to favour "facilitator" because it denotes more equal relations between educator and participants than some of the others. In choosing to use it we also recognize some potential problems. The word has been used to de-emphasize education as a political activity. For us, the facilitator is never "neutral".

Planning, for us, means the first steps in shaping an education event (who will come, where the session will take place, the resources needed). Unlike planning in traditional education, our planning means with rather than for people. Planning helps us think about the larger picture before we start to work on the design.

Designing best describes for us the decisions we make about the actual program for an event: its general framework, objectives, content, and process.

The **spiral design model** is a framework for designing educational events. The model stresses:

◇ starting with participant knowledge and experience
◇ bringing that experience into a collective framework
◇ adding new information and knowledge
◇ practising skills and forming strategies for action.

Practice is a word we use to describe our social, cultural, political, and educational activity; how we integrate our thinking and values into everyday action.

Democratic practice in our education work means maximizing the participation of those who are to benefit from our programs in the planning and design of the event as well as during the event itself. It means that in all of our activities we try to act in a way that is inclusive and maximizes participation in defining goals and activities.

Words about people

First Nations is what we understand to be the preferred term for referring to Canada's Native, aboriginal, or indigenous peoples by First Nations people themselves, and so we have tried to use that term wherever possible.

Minority refers to non-dominant racial or ethnic identities in Canada. While people with non-dominant (that is, non-European) ethnicities are numerically in the minority in Canada, they are not numerically in the minority in the world. (Globally, only 15 per cent of the world's population is White, of European heritage).*

Non-dominant or oppressed describes people or groups of people who have been denied power and legitimacy by virtue of their race, class, gender, age, sexual orientation, or ability.

People of colour is a term we use to apply to all people(s) who are not seen as White by the dominant culture. This includes Black, Native, Chinese, South Asian, Southeast Asian, Filipino, and Latin American Canadians. The term originates in the United States and is the one attempt by Black and Brown people to name themselves, not as "non-Whites" but as people with a positive identity. However, not all "people of colour" like the term. As one of our readers said, "This term has gained credence and is widely used. Personally, I think it's a way the dominant culture lumps the 'rest of them' together. For me it is the acceptance of the dominant view (as espoused by the dominant culture – white) that everyone else is 'people of colour'. I guess white isn't a colour."

Third World is the United Nations term used to describe the majority of the world's people in Africa, Asia, the Caribbean, and Latin America who have been exploited for centuries by the wealthier nations. The dislike that many so-called Third World people have for the "third class status" that the term denotes, as well as changes in the "second" (socialist) world, makes it a term very much in transition. We have used it in preference over developing nations, which assumes that "they" will become like "us". One alternative that is beginning to get wider use in the Third World is the geographic description North and South, which we have tried to use wherever we can, although this term too is not without its problems.

White: a social colour. We use the term, with an initial capital letter, to refer to people belonging to the dominant group in Canada. We recognize that there are many different people who are White but who face discrimination because of their class, gender, ethnicity, religion, age, language, physical abilities, or geographic origin. Grouping all these people as "White" is not to deny the very real forms of discrimination that people face because of the above factors. Nevertheless, in terms of physical appearance they may appear White in this society where this is the dominant social colour.*

* Barb Thomas, *Multiculturalism at Work: A Guide to Organizational Change.*

* Alok Mukherjee and Barb Thomas, "Bibliography on Racism, Anti-Racism and Educational Practice," mimeo, Toronto, 1990.

7

Acknowledgements

The writing phase of this project was co-ordinated by Bev Burke and the production by Barb Thomas.

The contribution of founding and current members of the DMI team has been essential. These are Deborah Barndt, Fran Endicott, Alfred Jean-Baptiste, Catherine Macleod, Alok Mukherjee, and Doris Marshall herself.

The manuscript was passed to ten colleagues who provided detailed and prompt comments that helped us greatly in the final draft. Our thanks to them all: Christine Almeida, Deborah Barndt, Carol Cayenne, Alfred Jean-Baptiste, dian marino, Alok Mukherjee, Denise Nadeau, Charlie Novogrodsky, Jeff Piker, and Lily Mah Sen.

Two tireless friends took on final production of the words and pictures in this book: our thanks to Robert Clarke for editing and Margie Bruun-Meyer for illustrations and design.

All photos and visuals are are credited where they appear.

Our intellectual and personal debt to popular educators in Southern Africa and Central America will be obvious. In particular, people in the Alforja network in Central America and in the Popular Education Working Group of the African National Congress have added clarity, vigour, and richness to our lives as well as our text.

The funding support provided by the Ontario Ministry of Skills Development has been instrumental in producing this book. Any royalties from sales will go to furthering the work of the Doris Marshall Institute.

Rick Arnold
Bev Burke
Carl James
D'Arcy Martin
Barb Thomas

Toronto, January 1991

1

This is our Chance:
Educating Strategically

6 LOOKING FORWARD: Implications for our work in the 1990's

5 LOOKING BACK: Issues emerging from our practice

 3 SHAPING OUR TOOLS: Developing and Using Activities

 2 WORKING BY DESIGN: Putting together a program

4 WORKING ON OUR FEET: The practice of democratic facilitation

1 THIS IS OUR CHANCE: Educating Strategically

This book is about the practice of education, and that practice includes, first of all, strategic preparation.

Whatever the context or the occasion, we want our work to make a difference. Whether we're chairing a meeting, planning organizational change, facilitating a workshop, creating a cultural production, or leading a mass rally, we aim to change power relations in the society, in however small a way.

That's because, for us, the status quo isn't neutral. Under the skin of our society there is pain. Increasingly, groups of Canadians are organizing around issues, both local (like the location of waste dumps) and international (like the negotiations for a free trade agreement among Canada, the United States, and Mexico). In these and other efforts to organize we are all nurturing a vision of a more just, humane society, in which creativity is encouraged and differences are respected.

At its best, education for social change gives us a taste today of what we seek in the future. The sessions can be varied and focused, humorous and serious. Our recipe for learning is equal portions of compassion, backbone, and curiosity. This heady mix sustains us through times of discouragement and draws us back to this work even when its effects seem diffused and slow.

Our commitment to education for social change, then, grows from a conviction that things should be different, a commitment to make them different, and a series of experiences that assure us that they can be different.

We have limited energies and skills and choosing the time and place to apply them is a matter of strategy. This chapter focuses on how to choose.

One possible choice is that education isn't what is needed. Let's face it, not all social ills can be remedied by workshops. As activist educators, we may conclude that organizing for direct action, or pausing for in-depth research, would be more appropriate than educational initiative. We must be prepared to problematize our own role, to consider the possibility of our own irrelevance at particular moments, if we are to make the most of the opportunities that really do present themselves.

For us, strategies for social change education rely on two initial steps. First we need to locate ourselves, and those with whom we work. Second we need to assess the situation around us. Only then can we start to push the limits of our social environment, to sharpen our tactical skills.

Many social activists prefer to skip the stage of locating themselves, so they can more quickly focus attention exclusively on the needs of a specific struggle. We believe that the needs of a struggle can only be met by people who are self-aware, sensitive to power dynamics, and engaged consciously with people different from themselves. In this spirit we direct our attention to social identity, organizational identity, and educational identity. We call this process "building critical self-knowledge".

The second step, assessing the situation, means considering how our identities have been moulded historically, rather than treating those identities as static and "personal". By analysing the context of our work, weighing up the balance of forces and the historical timing, our actions can have maximum effect.

DEBORAH BARNDT

Part of this, as we'll see, involves using the methodology of "Naming the Moment".

While researchers, organizers, and other allies can enrich our thinking, as educators we shouldn't absolve ourselves of social analysis. Strategic thought is too central to our work to be "contracted out". We have to do it for ourselves.

PAINTING
OURSELVES
INTO THE
PICTURE

We also need to start with ourselves. By this we mean that educators lacking critical self-knowledge can inadvertently erase themselves from the picture, by not working through basic questions about who they are and why they do what they do.

Usually it's during a break, when we are chairing a meeting or facilitating a course, that a participant poses the question directly. "Who are you, anyway?" The seriousness and honesty of our response depend on whether we've done our homework, whether we have reflected critically on our personal limits and potentials and on our social role.

Without critical self-knowledge, educators/activists can't face the challenge of social justice work effectively. If they don't clarify the different identities of educators, participants, and others, they will find that tensions arise unexpectedly and create problems rather than serve as a source of richness and creative energy.

If we can't put ourselves into the picture, we can't help others do the same. When the educator's personal identity and stake are made invisible, a learner can't quite pin down who is talking and what the person's connection is to the issue being discussed.

Most establishment education attempts to erase the educator – there is no subject to the verb. That's fine for the traditional power relations, where teachers dominate learners. As social change educators, refusing to erase ourselves isn't a matter of self-publicizing. It equips us to answer the legitimate questions from learners about who we are in relation to them and their issues.

Then the power dynamics in the group can be linked more consciously to the wider power relations in which our work is situated. We can make transparent the process of empowerment so that the learners can have informed and collective control over it.

The tool we use for locating the educator is an "identity triangle", made up of social identity, organizational identity, and political identity. Let's consider each dimension in turn.

The Identity Triangle

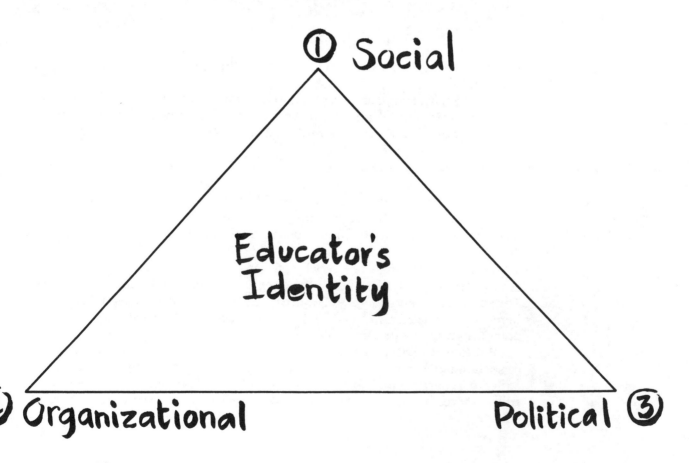

Social identity In our work we often use a graphic called the "power flower". It's a tool we use for looking at who we are in relation to those who wield power in society. We use the outer circle of petals (which a group usually fills in together) to describe the dominant social identity. The inner petals (which workshop participants fill by themselves or in pairs) describe the social identity of the individual.

The power flower is a versatile tool, and we will return to it again in other chapters of this book. For the moment, however, we want to use it to link the social identity of the educator and the people he or she works with.*

The Power Flower

Each "petal" of the flower represents – or names – an aspect of social identity. The blank petal is there to encourage people to add an aspect we may have omitted because of limits in our perception. Each petal can be used to situate the educator with regard to colleagues and participants, in a way that helps to predict where differences and tensions may emerge.

Two gay organizers conduct a workshop with parents in a neighbourhood school; members of a Vietnamese community organization invite an English-speaking theatre director to address their monthly meeting; a retired miner speaks with a group of working-class high-school students … the variations are almost endless. Our effort here is to develop self-awareness for strategic education.

* See chapter three, "DRAWING OUT KNOWLEDGE AND EXPERIENCE AND LOOKING FOR PATTERNS. The power flower: reflection on our social identities," for a detailed account of its use as a workshop activity. For a more comprehensive tool to analyse cultural influences on individuals, see Carl E. James, *Seeing Ourselves: Exploring Race, Ethnicity and Culture,* chapter I, particularly the diagram of concentric circles on p.16.

The politics of the gender petal

Let's take the gender petal, for instance. The gender makeup of a teaching team will influence, for better or worse, the kind of dynamics that are created in an educational activity, just because of the ways we have been socialized around leadership and gender.

A teaching team made up of a man and a woman will most likely find quite different dynamics than a team of two men or one with two women, particularly because of the power inequality between men and women in our society. But once the educators have acknowledged this inequality they can take steps in their program design to ensure that the woman's voice is built in equally from the start, and that bad habits of gender domination don't get reproduced throughout the process.

Once the educators deal with this issue, they have to consider their gender relations with the participants. Two women working together, if most of the group participants are male, have one challenge. Two men working together in a mixed-gender group have a different set of dynamics to consider. And so on.

Without making mechanical assumptions about behaviour based on gender, if we know the gender composition of the teaching team and the participant group we can make educated guesses beforehand about tensions that can arise. If, when we are planning events and workshops, we work through the power flower to identify differences and power inequalities that will affect the group dynamics, we enter the event equipped with that most valuable of assets: critical self-knowledge.

For instance, a male member of our team was once asked to co-teach a course in public speaking with a group of trade union women. The other teacher was a woman. For three days, in terms of gender, he was a minority of one, even though other parts of his social identity (race, union identification, language) formed bridges to the other participants. At a certain point in the discussion of gender politics it was clear that his gender had become an obstacle: it was preventing some of the less assertive women from voicing their feelings, partly because they didn't want him to be hurt by their anger. He had a choice to consider: to remain in the room and hence suppress the discussion, or to volunteer to leave for a couple of hours and return when his presence would no longer be a hindrance.

His behaviour was not at issue. This choice had nothing to do with his skill or his sympathy with women's rights. It was strictly a matter of his social identity and the power dynamics around it. Because of the pervasive violence against women, because patriarchal structures have silenced women, because of male-oriented pornography – the list could go on and on – there were intimate issues that union women simply couldn't broach with a man in the room. By consciously and explicitly choosing to leave in good humour, he ensured that the group could move ahead, and that he would be genuinely welcome back later to contribute in other areas of the course.

While it can be puzzling and anxiety-producing at times, this untangling of the personal from the structural can free educators as much as participants from dynamics that block learning.

The power of other petals

For each category of the power flower (age, gender, language, etc.) there is a dominant Canadian social identity.

We may be clear that in language the dominant identity is English and that in sexual orientation it is heterosexuality. But are we as clear about the implications of environmental thinking, the relations between humans and the natural environment? Are we in agreement about the dynamics among age groups or geographic regions? How often have we participated in meetings where differently abled people are fully integrated?

These identities have usually been built so deeply into our minds from an early age that we now take them for granted. We need to stop and probe our assumptions about them.

As educators we are continually surprised by the subtlety of these processes. Assumptions built in early in our lives have to be peeled away, layer by layer. Those of us engaged in educational work for social change need to probe the inequities that operate whenever a group of us gets together. We need to explore the diverse and pervasive ways in which inequities are reproduced and commit ourselves to overcoming them.

We must also be aware that this task is not always so straightforward. While class, race, and gender differences constantly emerge as central power dynamics, other petals of the power flower – religion or sexual orientation, for instance – are of decisive importance only on certain occasions. Deepening our consciousness about social identity requires taking time, probing our own discomfort, risking frank discussion.

No one is personally responsible for their social identity, but we are responsible for our actions. It doesn't help anyone if one of us feels guilty for being a Toronto-based, English-speaking educator in a workshop with Innu people in Labrador. On the other hand, it is crucial to be aware of the overriding privileges of central Canadian, English-speaking experience, and of how the group perceives such experience.

A failure to have this awareness will ensure failure in the workshop. An unwillingness to recognize – and learn about – the role of social identity will ensure the perpetuation of power relations and will hold back rather than advance the work of education for social change.

15

Organizational identity

The cultural approach

As educators, when we get involved with an organization, it's a package deal. With our affiliation comes entry into a subculture.

Think of how differently community service agencies, international solidarity committees, and trade unions operate day by day. Each of them has a code of how things are done, a collective memory with villains and heroes, a set of topics that make different people uncomfortable, an image of appropriate ways to celebrate and to mourn.

Those of us interested in political and ideological issues often underestimate the pervasive power of these cultures. As educators, we need access to the nooks and crannies of the organizational culture to work effectively with the organization.

There's a simple exercise that helps tune us in to this dimension of "organizational culture" in social action work. Look around the room at your meeting and ask yourself about each person you see who is attending on behalf of some organization. Do people from a particular organization have any distinctive ways of dressing or talking? Do they seem relaxed or rushed? Secure or nervous? Super-critical or ultra-diplomatic? Or is there anything else that sets them apart, or defines them?

Just by asking these questions you will begin to see the range of dynamics and practices embodied in our organizational identities.

Insiders and outsiders

In organizational cultures the most important dividing line is between insiders and outsiders. For instance, when we do education work within our own organizations we tend to have a certain dynamic. When an outsider comes in, the dynamic changes. As educators, when we work as outsiders the matter of who invites us in and how they present us to other members becomes of paramount importance.

Those of us who work as educational freelancers are constantly outsiders, a role that brings strengths as well as weaknesses in mixing with organizational cultures. When we're offered a job with an organization, we start by saying yes or no to the invitation. From the beginning, outsiders have to analyse organizational cultures as part of sorting out the potential and limits of the work.

For those of us who are insiders, employed within membership organizations like churches or unions, the issue of organizational culture has different implications. Often we have been members before moving into leadership roles and educational activity. Ours is the intimate knowledge of the "connected critic". Yet our insider status can make us unduly cautious. We might engage in a kind of self-censorship, toning down bold statements to the point where the organization might need to bring in an outsider for educational work.

When insiders and outsiders co-operate, they are crossing a line of organizational culture, whatever they may have in common in social identity and political stance. Both must be willing to share information and to continually negotiate the terms of alliance and the priorities.

Organizational cultures are reflected in language. Let's consider the names applied to people who conduct education sessions, for example. In schools they are called teachers, in universities they are professors, and in training institutions they are instructors. In social service organizations they are facilitators and in trade unions they are discussion leaders. There are also consultants, animators, chairs, and educators – the list goes on.

Sensitivity to language is essential for educators who want to make common cause with learners. One slip in a session – applying a label alien to the culture of the group, for instance – can take an educator from being part of a discussion to being perceived as "outside" or "other". It can happen in a moment, and the speaker may be blissfully unaware of what has taken place.

The best insurance against such slips, of course, is not a tense, self-conscious choice of words but an effort to make sure that the lines of communication at an event are always open – and not just two ways but in all directions – and that the "speaker" does not control these lines to her or his own advantage.

BARB THOMAS

17

Cultural mapping

Through our work, one organizational culture we've started to map from within is the Canadian trade union movement.* Our portrayal of the "union culture" emphasizes certain unifying features:

◇ it is essentially voluntary
◇ it shares important information verbally, not on paper
◇ it takes an adversarial position towards the corporate sector and government leadership
◇ it is internally politicized
◇ it maintains a tension between providing service and mobilizing members.

These five features could be explored in great detail, and certainly we could add more to the list. But even this short list is enough to help us begin to identify points of difference between unions and, let us say, community colleges, churches, social movements, or political parties.

In comparing "union culture" with "environmental group culture" we can consider how environmental groups function differently. For example, environmental groups tend to be:

◇ less hierarchical in their decision-making
◇ looser in their lines of internal accountability
◇ more flexible in forming tactical alliances on an issue-by-issue basis
◇ more influenced by formal academic research
◇ narrower in focus when lobbying government.

The comparison may be sketchy, but it's an example of a first stage in cultural mapping. When educators immersed in the processes of a women's collective enter a social service agency, or when someone experienced in policy work with senior adults enters an immigrant community organization, they must pay special attention to culture, to "how things are done around here". Certainly, we should not be surprised when tensions arise among organizations in a coalition, or when approaches and language that work in one location fail utterly in another.

The organizations we work with gradually influence our ways of speaking and acting. In the words of one seasoned trade unionist, "If you fly with the ducks long enough, you'll start to quack." As each of us begins an educational project, then, we need to be sensitive to organizational identities, our own and others, if we hope to communicate clearly and effectively.

* See D'Arcy Martin, "With A Little Help From Our Friends," in *Our Times*, Vol.VI, No.3 (April 1987); see also the *Our Times* issue on "Labour Education Today," Vol.V, No.1 (February 1986).

Political identity   Once we're clear on social identity and organizational identity, it's worth our while to talk about the political values in our educational work.

There is an enormous literature on adult education, and it's easy to become lost in it all. So we have grouped educational research and practice into three general political approaches: conservative, liberal, and transformational. Education activists can learn something from all these currents.*

Conservative approaches

The hegemony of the conservative current is backed up with extensive budgets, publications, scientific research teams, and references that are articles of faith, like "freedom" and "progress". The content of conservative education is the worldview and experience of the elites, which all others are expected to appreciate, if not emulate; and the function is ultimately to maintain the legitimacy of the status quo.

Within this current there is a certain continuum from traditional to technocratic thinking. At the traditional pole, conservative education is so nostalgic as to seem absurd, like the Afrikaner curriculum in Black South Africa's schools or the European and American "classics" that are studied to the exclusion of local literatures in colonies and neocolonies all over the world.

The more dynamic, technocratic pole equips a leadership for its ruling role and assigns the majority to their slots, the narrow tasks needed to reproduce the system. Under the guise of "hard facts", technocratic educators convince adult learners that those in charge belong there by virtue of their expertise, and that learners' choices need to be "realistic" within the framework of the status quo.

When modern productive systems began to polarize "good jobs" and "bad jobs", conservative educators responded with new content. They now speak of the need to overcome "critical skill shortages" as central to maintaining competitiveness, and they channel adult education resources to the "essential" workers in the top strata of the labour force. The priority for education is managing human resources to keep the economy ticking, and only when there is a surplus of educational resources will it be possible to educate the majority beyond a basic literacy level. In this approach the capitalist economy is a given, outside the realm of educators to question or challenge.

For conservative educators the U.S. psychologist B.F. Skinner is one of the key writers. The approach guides much of the competency-based training work by which workers are taught in Western Europe and North America. Among its expressions are the behaviour-modification exercises done by medical and counselling practitioners and the use of neuro-linguistic programming for sales and administrative personnel.

---

* For a balanced and comprehensive overview of the literature, see Stephen Brookfield, *Understanding and Facilitating Adult Learning.*

* See, for example, the highly successful training film, "The Hidden Advantage: Neuro-Linguistic Sales Programming," distributed in Canada by International Telefilm, Toronto.

The method of technocratic education is to trivialize or dismiss outright the life experience of learners. This requires labelling certain uses of language as correct, certain kinds of knowledge as valuable. When the social identity of the learners is different from the dominant group in race, class, gender, religion, or culture, they must be made to feel that their ideas are primitive and their aspirations "unrealistic". Then they will be fully open to the imposition of conservative education.

For all its negative impacts, one positive contribution of conservative education, largely at the technocratic pole, has been its insights into the non-verbal and unconscious dimensions of learning. This area has been exploited successfully by corporate and political advertisers, in particular. So far it has been addressed gingerly, if at all, by educators engaged in social justice work, because of the manipulative way that this research has been applied.

Liberal approaches

The second current, the liberal, draws on classical humanism, and among its more recent exponents are Malcolm Knowles in the United States and the late Roby Kidd in Canada. Within liberalism there is a continuum from personal to corporate thinking and practice. At the personal pole, liberals emphasize individualism, the self-directed learning of autonomous adults, with a measure of social reform. At the corporate pole are sophisticated organizational development ("O.D.") consultants and trainers, who work with major corporations and governments.

In liberal approaches the focus is on attitudes rather than structures, on the individual rather than the collectivity, on personal growth rather than political transformation.

The content of liberal education aims at developing the skills, confidence, and knowledge of the self-directed individual. With their great attention to attitudes, good liberal educators highly value the life experience of individual learners. They bring individual biographies and personal values into the core of the learning process. In this approach, education is neutral, stressing the need to look at both sides – and, less often, at all sides – of an issue.

In its method, liberal education focuses most fruitfully on the processes of self-directed learning and small group dynamics. The approach does have operational principles that can be useful to anyone in adult education, such as:

◇ making sure that participants understand that learning is valuable
◇ seeing mistakes as integral to learning
◇ drawing on and valuing the experience of participants
◇ connecting new facts or insights with what people already know
◇ building in direct and frequent feedback to the educator
◇ developing sensitivity to non-verbal forms of communication
◇ encouraging participants to take responsibility for their own learning.

Drawing on the humanist tradition of the well-rounded individual, corporate liberalism especially aims to develop a credible and fluent team member, within the existing social arrangements.

Liberal adult educators will undertake to improve unjust situations but avoid tackling the root causes of injustice. They emphasize the importance of "life skills", which oppressed people are expected to take up to change their self-defeating behaviours.

With knowledge as an essentially individual possession, liberal educators assert that its use should be subject to the free choice of each learner. Thus they allocate educational resources according to talent rather than wealth, with remedial programs offered to those who would not otherwise qualify. Within the curriculum, differences of gender, race, and class are respected, but there is no attempt to tackle the associated power inequities. Implicit here is a kind of paternalism, whereby education helps individuals to "rise above" their subordinate position.

The strength of this approach is its insight into human potential and individual diversity, and its resistance to manipulative teaching practices. The shift of emphasis in adult education from "knowledge in search of students" to "adults in search of knowledge" has been accomplished in many cases by dedicated and articulate liberal educators. As a result, liberals rarely assume that what is learned is what has been taught, which is a pitfall that conservative educators frequently tumble into.

For social change activists, the limitation of liberal approaches is their avoidance of power relations. The position that "education is neutral" reflects a resolute naivety in facing the fact that individuals are socially situated in an unequal world. As a result, many social activists are suspicious of the "touchy-feely" tone of liberal literature and dismissive of its potential contribution to building healthy organizations that can change the system.

While it is valuable at certain times to "look at both sides" of an issue or topic, this should be a step towards deepened commitment, not – as it often is – an excuse for inaction or a calculated blindness to oppressive and exclusive power structures. The tendency to ignore the broader power dynamics of learning situations means that liberal education is conveniently open to manipulation by those in power.

Transformational approaches

Educators connected to movements for radical democratic transformation work to link the goals of revolutionary politics with democratic practice and to build a variety of approaches to learning.

In the range of theory and practice there is a continuum from most participatory to most top-down or "vanguardist". In this book you will find us leaning towards the participatory end of the continuum.

In transformational approaches, education is part of a movement for individual and collective liberation, which promotes learning for critical consciousness and collective action. Such education seeks to transform power relations in society, relations between teacher and learner, and relations among learners. In this sense it is radically democratic.

The content of transformational approaches is the situation of oppression and the possible strategies for social change. The method begins with the lived experience of the learners, with validating it and exploring, through dialogue, its humanizing as well as oppressive dimensions. The method then moves to collective discussion about action, to the possibilities of transforming the oppressive elements of experience. This dynamic of reflection/action, or "praxis", is central to transformational approaches.

The intellectual root of the approach we have adopted in our educational work is in socialist and Third World liberation struggles. The key theorists include Paulo Freire of Brazil, Antonio Gramsci of Italy, and Julius Nyerere of Tanzania.

People involved in transformational approaches to education around the world use a number of terms that intersect with the growing international usage of "popular education". In Latin America, educators frequently refer to "educación popular" and "conscientizaçao", whereas in Southern and Eastern Africa the terms "people's education" or "education for self-reliance" are in common usage. In Asia, activists speak of "education for mass mobilization" and engage in "participatory research". In Europe we often hear of "cultural animation" work, while in Canada and the United States the insights of transformational education have influenced critical pedagogy, development education, feminist pedagogy, community-based adult literacy, as well as anti-racist and trade union education.

22

At the top-down pole are found some of our allies in specific struggles who draw on the brilliance of political economy writing by people such as Ernest Mandel and Louis Althusser and deduce their educational strategies from this starting point. These top-down transformational educators emphasize content over process and assert that correct theory in the heads of an enlightened few can translate into effective social justice work. Their downfall has been inattention to hierarchies and inequities in their own ranks, the sense of ignorance instilled in new recruits, and the sterility of debates among their leading intellectuals.

When, in reaction to top-down practices, the participatory pole leans too far in the opposite direction, it can merge into liberalism. But even at their clearest, participatory approaches have mostly been applied in small-scale initiatives. It's becoming clear, though, that we now need a new wave of thought to extend transformational education to challenges on a broader scale and to the educational opportunities that arise when oppositional movements actually win a measure of political power.

Our goal here is not to assert the primacy of a particular political "line" within education. Rather, we are proposing that political identity is integral to the critical and self-critical reflection of activist educators.

Once we have established this basic critical self-knowledge – locating ourselves in the triangle of social, organizational, and political identities – we are ready to assess the educational situations that all of us face. We have painted ourselves into the picture.

Political Identity: a summary sketch

EDUCATIONAL APPROACHES	PARTICIPANTS	THE GOALS
1. **CONSERVATIVE** * range from traditional to technocratic	* priority goes to those considered "essential" to the workforce	* effective leadership, pliable citizenry
2. **LIBERAL** * range from corporate to personal	* self-directed individuals seeking growth	* learners well adjusted * "neutral" on power issues
3. **TRANSFORMATIONAL** * range from participatory to "top down" * collective reflection and action	* oppressed people and those allied to their interests	* change power relations * transform socio-economic systems

ASSESSING THE
SITUATION

The purposes

Sometimes as educators we seem to be just plain wasting our time. Despite our deepest self-knowledge and our most skilful facilitation, we end up being in the wrong place at the wrong time – and it's usually because we didn't stop to consider the broader social context in the work.

If we aim to change power relations, we need to analyse those relations, to situate our work historically. That means careful social analysis.

Since our work aims at challenging existing power relations, our survival, not merely success, requires accurate and continual assessment of the social surroundings. At different times we may be building popular organizations, strengthening democratic impulses in liberal organizations, or stretching the margins of tolerance in conservative organizations. Each of these situations has different tactical imperatives. And, depending on the broader political and historical context, making choices and setting priorities will have a different flavour.

The key is power: we need to assess whose power moves things around us, and whose power we want to put our energy behind. At times, because we resist its current uses, we have to question our own ambivalence about power. In addition to ensuring the material basis for our own survival, we need to review what work and which participants will help produce the changes that we are committed to.

In these very practical, day-to-day ways, we need our own brand of social analysis. We know that this analysis doesn't have to be solitary and competitive, as it is so often in a career-oriented society. Nor does it have to be abstract and dry, like so much academic political economy. We can draw on the collective knowledge that groups have gained through struggles around a variety of issues. And we can share that knowledge, with less critique – in the sense that we want to move beyond critique to making proposals for alternatives – and more proposal, less overview and more strategy.

Our purpose in social analysis is to assess the momentum of the forces around us and thereby formulate our own priorities. In the words of Sun Zi, written in 500 B.C.:

> The inherent speed of rushing water uproots boulders. This is due to momentum. The unerring sweep of the diving falcon gets the prey. This is due to judgment. Momentum is like the pent-up force in the cross-bow, judgment is like the sudden release of the trigger. A skillful fighter is one whose momentum is invincible and whose judgment is accurate.*

* Tang Zi-Chang, *Principles of Conflict*, recompilation and new English translation with annotation on Sun Zi's art of war (San Rafael, Cal.: T.C. Press, 1969), pp.36-37.

We should expect opposition from those in power to the ideas we are promoting. Without adopting the militarism of Sun Zi, we should expect, in all serenity, to struggle. We cannot do that effectively without rigorous social analysis.

We also need to keep our purposes clear to sustain ourselves in educating for social change. This work requires nourishment, which social vision can help to provide. Part of social analysis, then, is creative. It means constantly refining and updating the ideas of economic justice, political democracy, or pro-feminist and anti-racist process, and extending these ideas both in our lives and in the society around us.

The content The content of social analysis is possibilities, their shape and extent. We can develop technical skills as educators, in planning, design, and facilitation of learning events. But uncovering the power relations that are part of and surround an event requires a grasp of different content, in four main areas.*

✦ The first area of content concerns the **identities and interests** of the people we are working with. This draws directly on the three dimensions of identity: social, organizational, and political.

Consider, for example, an invitation to do a weekend workshop on social action with a church congregation in Sydney, Nova Scotia. Naming the social identities involved, using all the petals of the power flower, is the starting point for placing this opportunity in context and assigning it some priority.

For a start, we ask if the congregation includes working people and unemployed people, with a range of involvements in the social action traditions of Cape Breton. Secondly, we assess our own organizational identity, in particular the nature and strength of our alliances in that region. Then we examine our political identity as well as the political identity of the people issuing the invitation.

This type of process happens continually. With each new social action, with each educational event, we are challenged in new ways to look at who we are and what our underlying interests are, as well as at the social identity of the other participants in the action or event.

In deciding whether or not to accept such an invitation we need to recognize that, unless educators are to become a private club, we must reach out constantly to include people beyond our own social and organizational network. We need to broaden our sense of potential allies, groups, and people who share our interests and can enrich our vision.

---

* In this section, and indeed in the balance of this chapter, we owe much to the work of the "Naming the Moment" group in Toronto. Deborah Barndt, a founding member of the Doris Marshall Institute, has co-ordinated this group since its beginning, and other members of the DMI team have worked in particular roles as the Moment process has unfolded. See in particular the manual for community groups, edited by Deborah Barndt, *Naming the Moment: Political Analysis for Action.* See also *The Moment,* published three times a year, each time highlighting a particular issue. The Summer 1990 issue (Vol.IV, No.1), for example, deals with the Canadian federal government's Goods and Services Tax.

Along the way we need to clarify who's with us both in the short term and the longer haul. In deciding who we're going to work with, subjective factors also come into play. Who do we enjoy? Who challenges us? We like to look for elements of warmth, surprise, and fun in our working relationships.

Most people we know do much the same. They attend events, accept invitations, volunteer for assignments because they like the people they'll be working with. This personal, subjective side of judgement is less systematic, somehow less "political" and hence less often discussed publicly. But all of us draw upon it as an element of common sense and nourishment in doing our work over the long term.

✦ The second area of content, **naming the issues,** requires focusing on "what matters" in the welter of concerns around us. Paulo Freire calls this "identifying the generative themes".

These themes or issues are the arenas of greatest struggle at a particular moment, the most critical social tensions. Not surprisingly, they offer the greatest potential for developing consciousness and building organization.

Using the Sydney example, we'd have to search for a preliminary sense of the social concerns in the church congregation. Is regional unemployment on their agenda? Are the militant union traditions of the area a source of pride or shame? Discussion of these matters needn't be narrowly bound by political economy. What is called for is a capacity to integrate emotional and intuitive knowledge into our inquiry. To use only the left side of the brain is to use only half our intelligence, individually and collectively.

RICK ARNOLD

26

✦ The third area of content is **assessing the forces.** This requires a clear view of the dominant agendas, and an unsentimental synthesis of popular agendas. It is essential that we know the strengths and weaknesses of both sides – intellectually, organizationally, and politically – before we leap into discussion processes.

The question to raise about the Sydney workshop would concern the individual and collective leverage of congregation members – or their willingness – to address the generative themes. Without this leverage a workshop could still result in some new ground being broken, but it would more likely raise the level of disappointment and frustration in people who are not able to act on the issues raised.

This part of the analysis requires "street smarts", particularly in identifying weaknesses in the dominant structures – what radical educator and artist dian marino calls the "cracks in consent". It might be good, for instance, to suggest that the workshop include joint participation with other social action groups in the community, rather than be limited to the congregation.

✦ The fourth content area in social analysis is **planning for action.** If we've taken care to follow the first three steps, this one will logically follow. And weighing the possible courses of action will be the final test in deciding whether or not to accept an invitation for the workshop.

This often means applying the weapon of imagination to the task, trying to turn "hindrances" into "helps". What is the "free space" that this occasion offers, the opportunities for action created by the particular relationship of forces we can see in operation?

In the hypothetical case of the Sydney church congregation, we know – or find out – that there is no place in Canada with a more fully documented history of popular struggle than Cape Breton Island. We'd need further research and discussion to locate the current possibilities for action in the flow of past action.

Taking a broader perspective, we want to urge the integration of educational work within the context of social and political organizing. We see a link between the learning that can be harvested from organizing a rally and the research and organizing generated from an educational event. The connections between education and politics, then, are reciprocal, and they operate at both the conceptual and organizational levels.

By introducing these four steps in the content of social analysis, as a proposal for sorting out educational opportunities, we are, again, adapting material developed by the "Naming the Moment" group. We are also anticipating a sequence that will be explored in more depth when it comes to actually designing the educational event.

This kind of continual social and political analysis helps us make planning decisions, but it also becomes integral to educational design and facilitation. We can encourage the groups we work with to respond more strategically, in part by modelling such behaviour ourselves, not just by proposing it in workshops.

This, then, is our agenda for the content of social analysis. It is not a conventional set of research priorities. Nor do we consider that all four areas must be exhaustively covered before beginning educational work. But keeping these four sets of concerns in our minds as we work is essential to using our scarce financial and human resources for maximum social effect.

The method   All of us make time for solitary research, through reading for instance, but that's only a part of social analysis. We have also tried to develop methods of analysis consistent with the ways we educate. This involves engaging with others, creating analysis with others, celebrating discovery of ideas, acknowledging that struggle is a teacher. It's a lot more diverse and rich, we find, than your average reading list.

In particular, we want to emphasize the importance of broadening the in-crowd of sources for social analysis. When dealing with organizations, this means listening to the people at the bottom of the heap.

Try answering the phone in an office for a while. See how you feel when a caller asks "Is anyone there?"

Sometimes it's a shock how little traditional hierarchies have really changed, even in groups that attempt to play a role in radical social change. Clerical employees in unions, blue-collar workers in universities, food service employees at social change conferences: these people have a particular vantage point on the substance, and the hollowness, of social change practices. It's worth taking the time to listen to what they know, and not be limited to the insights of the "movers and shakers" in social change work.

Within organizations, the fact that one person's position is higher than another's doesn't necessarily mean that the "superior" person has more knowledge. Indeed, both from visceral identification with the underdog and from experience of what knowledge is needed to change things, we are probably safer to assume the opposite.

Ours is a politics of inclusion. In broadening out we need to keep in mind the discussion of identity. We seek to "keep difficult company", by which we mean including those whose social, organizational, and educational identities can be a persistent source of challenge.

When we're organizing an event, we might review the power flower petals with regard to our planning team and find out if there are social identities that we've excluded in the process.

Similarly with organizational identities, we can seek to include both insiders and outsiders and to make sure that our event has representation from a full range of skills and levels in the hierarchy.

As for political identities, the question here is to judge when the basic goals of the event are clear enough and broadly enough supported that inclusion of other political perspectives won't sabotage the process.

When we engage with people over a sustained period we need a more structured method for continuing social analysis. In our view, the most consistent and highly developed tool for this purpose is the "Naming the Moment" approach. The Toronto-based group of social change educators and activists that has developed the tool began in the tradition of "conjunctural analysis", particularly as developed in Latin America. Over a period of years they have developed a flexible, participatory, imaginative process, suited particularly to the needs and cultures of popular organizations in Canada. The group already has connected with the struggles of First Nations, neighbourhood organizations, coalitions, refugees, and trade unionists.

Within the Doris Marshall Institute (DMI) team we have identified four great strengths in the Moment method. First, the approach is comprehensive. The approach helps us to see what makes a situation an opportunity, providing the elements of timing and readiness that are so often lost in more detached social analysis approaches.

Second, the method is dynamic. It is not locked into an economism, for example, which would suppress the cultural dynamics in situations, or into a static emphasis on structures that begs the question of how change can happen.

Third, the method is inclusive. The experience and insight of those directly engaged in social action work carry the same weight as those who observe it. People of different social, organizational, and educational identities can all contribute to a total picture, which they then all "own".

DEBORAH BARNDT

EDUCATING FOR A CHANGE

Fourth, and last, it is fun. The process of linking insights, of sharing moments of "Ah-Hah!", generates energy rather than saps it, and it builds community rather than withdraws from it.* This is partly because the Toronto Moment group has developed expressive exercises of all sorts to engage intuitive and holistic thinking. Group members don't limit themselves to conventional linear or even dialectical logic.

While the Moment method is effective, it too is constantly evolving. Participants challenge its cultural and class biases and creatively adapt it to use with new groups of activists. We encourage readers to consult the Moment publications and to consider this discussion as a springboard for developing more rigorous and participatory social analysis in the course of educational work.

In the end the method we choose for social analysis is linked to our educational values. Similarly, we must align the objectives we set in education and the purposes of the social analysis we engage in as a part of the process. Planning assumes that we are positioned to act, to do the possible – and then to push out the limits.

* GATT-Fly, *Ah-Hah! A New Approach to Popular Education.*

2
Working by Design
Putting Together a Program

6 LOOKING FORWARD: Implications for our work in the 1990's

5 LOOKING BACK: Issues emerging from our practice

3 SHAPING OUR TOOLS: Developing and Using Activities

2 WORKING BY DESIGN: Putting together a program

4 WORKING ON OUR FEET: The practice of democratic facilitation

1 THIS IS OUR CHANCE: Educating Strategically

An educator from Ontario accepts an invitation to lead a bilingual workshop in Quebec with participants from all over Canada representing a range of sectors and issues. The workshop, within a larger conference, is to move towards recommendations for future coalition work.

As the educator begins to think about the session, her "nightmare" takes shape. She arrives at the session and tries to introduce the program and objectives in both languages. Irate, the Québécois participants demand a new facilitator who speaks good French. Somehow she struggles on, but as they finish the morning's work, a prominent male trade union leader in the group confronts her: "This is a waste of time – all this 'popular education' nonsense. I've had it!" He walks out, joined by most of the participants.

It isn't surprising that this work gives us nightmares. As social change educators, we care passionately about what we do. But often we don't take ourselves seriously enough. We forget that our work is a craft, and that it is a risky one, with extremely high stakes.

We're on the front line, dealing with people's dreams, fears, and sometimes their livelihoods. That makes it all the more important to tackle our "nightmares" in advance, through planning and design.

RICK ARNOLD

32

The politics and economics of planning

Planning and design can help our educator deal with the nightmare in Quebec before it has a chance to happen. She takes some French lessons to brush up her language skills. When they design the workshop, she and her co-facilitator build in time during the workshop agenda to share their expectations with the participants and to have ongoing critical reflection on the process. If they get critical feedback during the sessions they can stop and redesign what's happening to fit the need.

Often, the organizations we work for don't place much importance on this part of our craft, and advance planning is minimized by educators themselves. The same person who spends a good deal of time carefully planning a three-hour speech will walk into a discussion with little or no prior planning, to "sit and rap". There is a clear political position embedded in this behaviour. It suggests that the words of the person delivering the speech are more important than the many voices in the discussion.

A major problem with planning and design is that it is hidden work. This creates an economic problem where educators within organizations are not given sufficient time to plan, and outsiders are almost never paid for all of the time they put into the design of an event. The result for the educators is overload. With too many sessions and other competing interests, planning becomes a luxury we aren't sure we can afford.

It's also important to spell out the workshop design on paper, and provide this as a handout to participants at the meeting, probably at or towards the end. This technique, of making sure workshop participants see process as something constructed, is another element that helps us take control of our own learning.

Those of us committed to democratic education practice cannot afford not to spend the necessary time planning and designing our work.

Why we spend time planning:
✧ to show respect for people
✧ to ensure better use of time and resources
✧ to avoid the temptation to talk at people
✧ to begin to deal with our nightmares
✧ to help ensure control of the process by participants
✧ to ensure co-ordination with co-facilitators
✧ to build participant interests and concerns into the program
✧ to structure activities that maximize participation
✧ to build in optional activities that can be used to redesign the program or agenda during the session itself.

And here's why we provide a written description of the workshop design:
✧ to make the process of the event visible to the participants
✧ to share our ideas and experiences with other educators
✧ to help evaluate the plan afterwards
✧ to have material for use in future programs.

A note on planning, design, and facilitation

Let's look again at how our educator tried to deal with her nightmare. Among other things, she took French lessons as part of the planning, before the workshop. In designing the workshop, she included time for the participants to stop and critically reflect on what was happening. (Later, when she did critical feedback at the end of the first morning, she was able to take time during the lunch break to redesign the rest of the workshop to meet the needs of the participants.) All of this helped her to work on her feet during the actual facilitation of the session.

After a course on democratic educational practice with the African National Congress (ANC) in Lusaka, Zambia, workshop participants helped us come up with a graphic to illustrate the different aspects of planning, design, and facilitation:

What do we mean by planning, design, and facilitation?

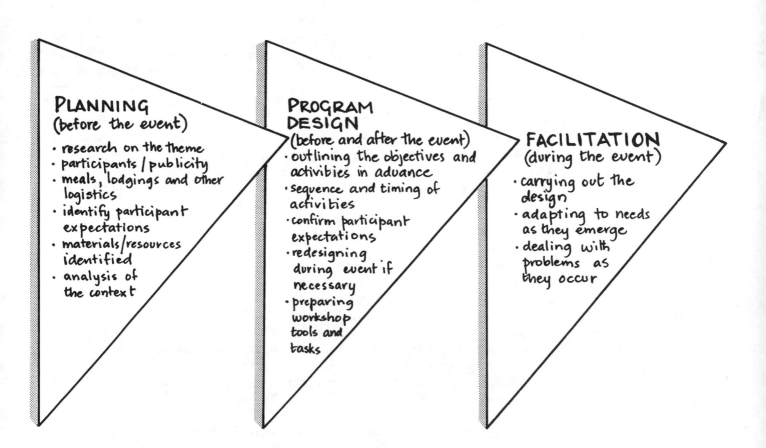

PLANNING
(before the event)
- research on the theme
- participants / publicity
- meals, lodgings and other logistics
- identify participant expectations
- materials/resources identified
- analysis of the context

PROGRAM DESIGN
(before and after the event)
- outlining the objectives and activities in advance
- sequence and timing of activities
- confirm participant expectations
- redesigning during event if necessary
- preparing workshop tools and tasks

FACILITATION
(during the event)
- carrying out the design
- adapting to needs as they emerge
- dealing with problems as they occur

The planning phase

You arrive at the room to be used for your workshop only to discover that the room is locked. When you locate the janitor with the key you discover that the room has only one outlet and you need an extension cord. The slide-tape program is key to your design so you take the time to find the janitor again – and begin late. Part of the way through the showing, the projector bulb burns out, and you have no spare.

Or: you get to a workshop and find out only too late that small juice packs and styrofoam cups are the only containers available, which means trouble because these containers are not environmentally acceptable.

Sound familiar? In these situations, the educators hadn't looked at the room in advance, checked the equipment, or considered how the refreshments would work. And it always seems that what we forget to do in the planning phase comes back to haunt us during the event itself. Based on our own past nightmares, here are a few things we think about before the event, in the planning phase.

35

A planning checklist

In the checklist we're leaving a space under each item so you can add other points.

Participants ■ participants selected
■ advance information to participants on program/logistics
■ advance information from participants on expectations
■ information about participants and their expectations
■

Context ■ sponsoring organization(s) identified
■ advance information on sponsoring organization(s)
■

Resources ■ funding secured
■

Logistics ■ book place, equipment, audio-visuals
■ organize meals, coffee/juice breaks (keeping the environmental factors in mind)
■ purchase supplies such as flip-chart paper, non-toxic marker pens
■ check room(s) in advance for:
❑ outlets and curtains for A.V. equipment
❑ space for large- and small-group work
❑ wall space for posting flip-chart paper, chairs, tables
❑ ways to adjust heat, light, ventilation
■

Materials ■ photocopy handouts, tasksheets
■ organize booktable/displays
■

Documentation ■ decide how to document event
■ get the equipment/supplies required for documentation
■

The design phase: the model matters

What we understand by "education" is reflected in how we carry out our work. To illustrate this point, we're going to take a look at two models.

One of us "researched" the first model while flying back to Canada from work in another country. He was amazed to find a proposed system for designing learning experiences amongst the glossy literature on the airplane.* He found an ad for what's known as the "banking" model of education, a part of the conservative-technocratic stream of education. The model looked like this.

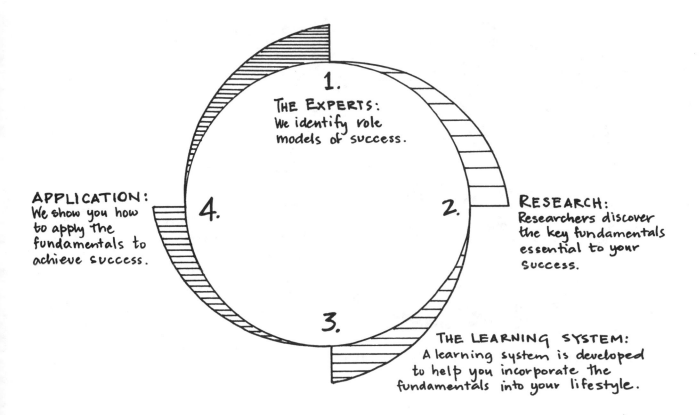

1. **THE EXPERTS:** We identify role models of success.

2. **RESEARCH:** Researchers discover the key fundamentals essential to your success.

3. **THE LEARNING SYSTEM:** A learning system is developed to help you incorporate the fundamentals into your lifestyle.

4. **APPLICATION:** We show you how to apply the fundamentals to achieve success.

This model suggests that:

1. learning begins with the experts, who are our role models;
2. teachers have the information consumers need to succeed;
3. success means conforming to the role model, which means becoming like the experts; in other words, supporting the status quo.

* American Airlines, "Sybervision", ad on inside cover, Winter 1990. For a model within the "liberal" stream, see J. William Pfeiffer, ed., *A Handbook of Structured Experiences for Human Relations Training*, Vol. IX (California: University Associates, 1983), especially the Introduction, pp. 1-3.

In planning for a workshop together, three of us pooled our own best attempts at design models. We came up with one we call "the spiral model", which we now use in our work.

The spiral model

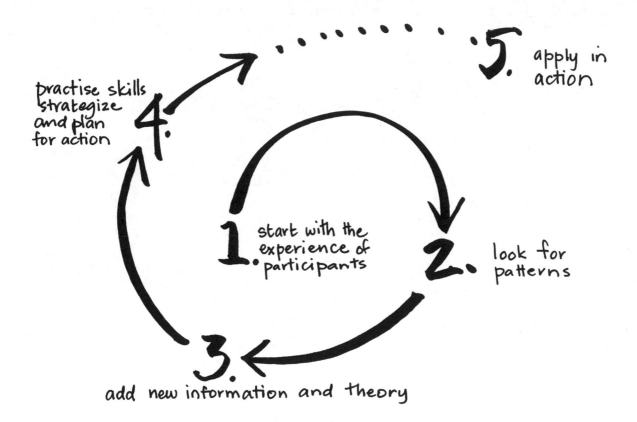

This model suggests that:

1. learning begins with the experience or knowledge of participants;
2. after participants have shared their experience, they look for patterns or analyse that experience (what are the commonalities and what are the differences?);
3. to avoid being limited by the knowledge and experience of people in the room, we also collectively add or create new information or theory;
4. participants need to try on what they've learned: to practise new skills, to make strategies and plan for action;
5. afterwards, back in their organizations and daily work, participants apply in action what they've learned in the workshop.

An extension of this model is that later participants return to share the experience for further assessment and critique, and perhaps work to revise the strategies – moving through the cycle again.

What happens when we compare the assumptions in the spiral model with those in the expert model?

◇ The spiral model values not only the knowledge and experience of the outside expert, but also – and even more – the knowledge and experience of the participants.

◇ In the spiral model everyone teaches and everyone learns in a collective process of creating new knowledge, rather than only the teacher teaching and the students learning using the expert model.

◇ In the spiral model, education leads to action for social change, rather than to the maintenance and reproduction of the status quo.

Why we find the spiral model useful

✦ **The spiral model helps us work with creative tensions.**

a) tension between practice and theory

We began designing and facilitating education programs by the seat of our pants. It was only in reflecting on our own education practice that we realized we needed some theory. We learned from books and other experiences, including those in Central America. This learning led us to develop our own approach, the spiral model.

This is not the usual approach to developing theory. In school we learned that theory is something developed by the experts, something that usually seemed quite unrelated to day-to-day living and working. In contrast, we are suggesting that theory involves going down into a deeper understanding of our own day-to-day existence, rather than up into the abstract. *

So theory not only informs our practice but it also springs from it. In this way we are all theorists.

b) tension between action and reflection

Have you ever noticed how often social activists complain about having no time? In our result-oriented, "time poor" culture, time for reflection (or thinking) is not only limited but also often seems a waste of time. The spiral model helps introduce a dynamic relationship, between action and reflection, into the design of an educational event.

The starting point is experience (past actions). We reflect on and learn from this experience to develop new action plans for the future.

c) a tension between participant knowledge and new input

In our society, because we are taught to trust the experts, we don't usually learn to value lived experience as a source of knowledge.

In one trade union workshop, for example, an organizer shut off the video camera during a session when workers were talking about their experiences with a health and safety problem; and turned it on again when the U.S. expert arrived to deliver her presentation.

* Thanks to Oscar Jara of Alforja in Central America for the concept of "profundización" (deepening).

In contrast, the spiral model places a great deal of value on participant knowledge. Indeed, it links new input to the experience of participants.

✦ **The spiral model takes into account how people learn.**

THE LEARNING HEADS

| hear only | see only | hear and see | hear, see, talk | hear, see, talk and do |

% we retain

20%   30%   50%   70%   90%

We use the learning heads in some of our workshops to demonstrate that people retain more of what they learn when they use more of their senses and can apply what they are learning. The work of some academics in the field of non-verbal learning – while we often have serious reservations about how this work has been applied – has helped us understand more about how people learn. The spiral model allows us to use this new information in the way we structure our education sessions.

✦ **The spiral model uses what we know about effective adult education.**

Principles of effective adult education practice
or
How we know effective adult education is happening*

- participants see what they are learning as valuable
- the goals are clear
- participants can make mistakes
- the experience of all participants is valued and drawn upon
- new facts and insights are connected to what participants already know
- participants get direct and frequent feedback
- people share/debate/discuss what they are learning with others
- participants feel respected/listened to
- participants have input into how teaching and learning happens
- differences in identity and experience are acknowledged

* Adapted from the Canadian Labour Congress, *Instructor Training Course Manual* (Ottawa: Canadian Labour Congress, 1983), with the additional input of Anne Marie Stewart and Barb Thomas.

But this list is not enough for social change educators. Although effective adult education has a lot to teach us about how people learn and we use these principles in our work, they are just the first step.

✦ The spiral model incorporates the principles of Education for Social Change.

Deborah Barndt, an author and popular educator based in Toronto, talks about a friend who once said: "I find it dangerous to know HOW to do something without knowing WHY and FOR WHOM." The expert learning model trains people to adapt – to fit better into society as it is. Education for social change has a radically different goal.

As social change educators, we add to the principles of good adult education.

Principles of education for social change
or
How we know education for social change is happening

Social change education:

- critically examines unequal power relations, not just differences (race, class, gender, disability, heterosexism, ageism)
- names and challenges ideas and practices that support inequality
- anticipates and addresses conflict
- encourages creative expression
- uses the mind, hands, and emotions
- is a continuing process, not a single event
- strengthens organization
- encourages collective action for change
- models democratic relations between learner and leader
- includes both reflection and action
- puts local issues into national and global contexts

Education for social change is NOT neutral.

THE BUILDING
BLOCKS

In putting together a program design, we ask ourselves a number of questions about the educational session: these questions and answers become our building blocks.

In our workshops with other educators, we often have participants talk about and then dramatize their nightmares about doing community education work. Here is one example:

A community centre servicing a largely immigrant community asks two immigrant women to facilitate a workshop on the issue of violence against women. The two women arrive early, set the chairs in a circle, and put their notes up on a flip-chart. When the participants – both men and women – arrive, they hesitate to sit in the circle but finally agree to do so.

As the facilitators begin it soon becomes evident that some participants speak no English and will need translation. When they've completed their introduction to the agenda, one of the men raises a hand to say that there is no violence against women in his community and he is opposed to this meeting. When the facilitators ask if anyone disagrees, there is silence.

Steering around our nightmares: who's coming and why

What prior information could have helped these educators manoeuvre around this situation?

In our experience, there are four important elements to think about before beginning to work on the design: the participants, things to guard against, the desired outcomes, and the resources and skills we have or need to get. A worksheet that we use in our skillshops for educators summarizes these questions.

✦ **the participants**

Some of the information we try to have in advance includes:

■ gender, race, ethnic background, class, age, sectors, or areas of work
■ first language/fluency in the language to be used in the session
■ if/how well they know each other
■ what experience they have with the topic
■ what attitudes, understandings, skills they are likely to bring
■ why they are coming

42

Worksheet: Thinking About Your Event

As the first stage in our design we work through these questions.

Total time available:

Title of your event _____

Participants: What do you know (and not know) about participants attending your event? i.e. gender, race and ethnic background, first language, social class, age, sectors, areas of work; will they know each other's names; what is their experience with the topic; what attitudes, understandings, skills are they likely to bring to the workshop? Why are they coming?

Things to guard against or your worst scenario

What resources / skills do you have which will help you do this?
What do you have to get?

Setting some objectives

a) What specifically do you want participants to feel, know, understand, be able to do at the end of your event?

b) Identify 3 specific objectives for your event.

✦ things to guard against – your worst scenario
This is the moment to think about our nightmares. If we identify them in advance we can take them into account, possibly avoid them. In the example of the workshop on violence against women, we could have foreseen the possibility of challenge by a male participant and discussed and practised several responses.

We do want to stress, though, that in the design we are trying to look for ways to explore tensions creatively, not to flatten or avoid them.

✦ resources and skills we bring/need to get
In our design we identify ourselves in relation to the group and the issue, using the identity triangle introduced in chapter one.

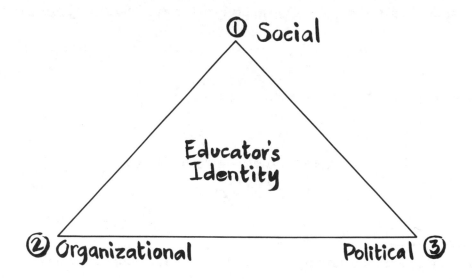

Our two educators recognized that while they shared the same race and ethnic background (social identity) as most of the participants, their perspective on the issue was radically different. As outsiders to the community organization (organizational identity), they began to think about how to involve some of the participants in the planning process so they could together explore appropriate ways of introducing the issue of violence against women.

✦ desired outcomes: what we want people to feel, know, understand, be able to do at the end of the session
The educators needed more advance information about desired or anticipated outcomes. The community organization that issued the invitation might have been asked to name a planning committee to meet with the educators. At the meeting, the planning group would have had a chance to clarify what they wanted from a session on violence. Why were they organizing the event?

Then, if anyone challenged the basic purpose of the event, members of the planning committee would have been in a position to help the facilitators deal with the situation.

44

Getting the objectives straight

Having found out who's coming, formulating some desired outcomes, and discussing things to guard against and the resources we need to bring, we begin to set more specific objectives.

In our workshops with educators there are always audible groans when we get to this part. Setting objectives is not easy for any of us. Yet we've found it to be the most important part of the design process. Setting clear objectives really helps us all to be clearer about what we want to do. Once we have the objectives, it's easy to do the rest of the planning.

So, once the groans have subsided, we do an exercise that first asks people to divide into planning teams and fill in the "Worksheet: thinking about your event". In setting objectives, the first question we ask the educators to think about is what they want participants to feel, know, understand, and be able to do at the end of the event – a stage that is a process tool for generating objectives.

After this discussion the task becomes a matter of identifying three specific objectives for the event. Once this is done we come back together and ask one group to volunteer their work. Using the following guidelines, we rework the objectives together.

Guidelines for setting objectives
◆ Are they realistic for the time you have?
◆ Is there a clear verb that suggests an activity?
◆ Is the objective measurable? How would you know if you had done this?
◆ Is it appropriate to the group? i.e., could you express this objective to the group and get support for it?
◆ Is there a logical flow from one objective to the other? (refer to stages of the spiral design model)
◆ Do the objectives address what you want people to feel, know, and be able to do?

RICK ARNOLD

EDUCATING FOR A CHANGE

An example

After using the worksheet, one planning team volunteered their objectives for the full group to revise.

✦ original objectives

1. critically reflect on our own individual experiences of learning
   The changes included use of verbs that suggested activities; making the objective more specific, keeping in mind the time available.

2. draw out and analyse principles of social change education.
   Here there was a problem with the flow from #1 to #2 – in that you could not analyse what had not yet been introduced.

3. identify the aims of union education.

✦ revised objectives

1. describe and discuss our own experience of learning in union educational events

2. draw out and introduce principles of social change education

3. develop guidelines for the aims and organization of union educational events.

Using the flow of the spiral model as the planning guide, objective #3 needed to move towards some action or strategy, in this case policy guidelines for the union.

PUTTING THE
PIECES
TOGETHER

Imagine that we're taking the next step in designing an educational program – a workshop – together. We've broken the workshop up into its separate pieces: we know who's coming, and why, we've considered all the angles we could think of, and we've set our objectives.

Now it's time to put the pieces back together, which for us is the most creative and fun part of advance planning. At this point, keeping in mind the stages of the spiral model, we add a number of elements critical to any successful education event.

✦ getting started
In considering the design of our workshop, we note the tasks we will need to take care of at the outset of the event, such as introductions, finding out why people are there, discussing the agenda and objectives.

✦ reflection
We place "reflection" in the middle of the diagram to indicate that we want to build reflection and evaluation into the design all the way through – not just leave them until the end.

Stages of a workshop

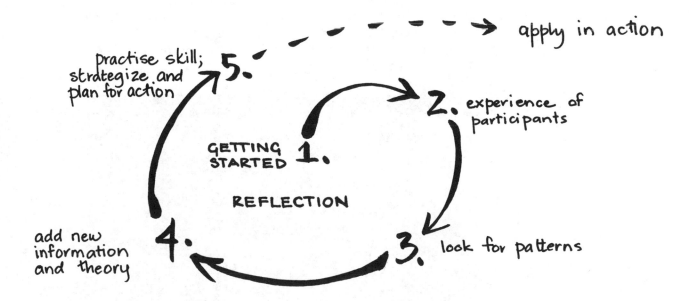

Now let's move on to look at each stage of our design. We'll be talking about why we've found each stage important and about some of the problems we've faced. We'll share some tips on how to deal with these problems. In the next chapter we'll outline some of the activities that can be used at each moment in the design.

Getting started

One of the most frightening times in a workshop for the facilitator – and sometimes for the participants as well – is the first few minutes. You face a group you don't know. The group always seems larger than it really is, and the faces blur. If you're a participant you worry, "Oh no, this is going to be a waste of time." Or you're afraid you'll embarrass yourself somehow. So as educators, what we do in the first ten minutes is significant in setting the tone for the entire event.

We also know that first impressions are powerful. If we wow them in the first ten minutes, we can always coast until at least the end of the first activity! Joking aside, the issue of credibility is particularly vital for an outsider to the organization. It is a paradox in democratic education practice that before you can successfully give over control to the participants, you need to establish your credentials, to get their respect.

The mistake we most often make is not spending enough time in building relations among people in our events. When we don't take this necessary time, we find that we pay for it part way through. As social change educators, we see our role as providing support for the building of a movement for social change. Building trust in and among organizations within the movement is an important part of that role. To build trust takes time.

We have also found that it is important, though, to balance this need with the needs of task-oriented participants who want to see some hard content early on. In a shop-stewards course on grievance procedures, for example, participants will be anxious to start getting into aspects of dealing with the grievances of co-workers. If you start with too many group-building activities the level of impatience and anxiety in the room is going to build up – and perhaps come crashing down. So decisions about how much of what kind of activity to introduce depend on the particular organizational culture of participants (a concept we talked about in chapter one).

MARGARET MCCOLL

What to do in the first hour

The most basic task for beginning is that of introductions – people need to find out enough about each other and the workplan to feel comfortable. Also, to give people time to "get there" as part of our introductions, we ask them to talk about what they had to do to get to the event.

✦ **Establish your credibility.** For example, two of us who are not trade unionists were asked by the education director of a major union to do a session on popular education. We were not only outsiders to the union and the province, but we would also be presenting what might be considered suspect subject matter. After talking to the union members who had invited us, we decided to start by giving participants a sense of who we were. So we presented ourselves more formally than usual. We also got the union president to lend a little extra credibility to the proceedings by introducing the session and us to the members. In any session it is critical to let people know who you are and how you connect with them.

✦ **Find out why people are there.** Even when you've collected information in advance, all participants are rarely involved in the planning so there is a need to check expectations to make sure that the plan is going to meet their needs. This stage also lets people hear directly from each other and gives out the message that the intent is to make this workshop their program, not ours. We often put people's expectations down on paper, providing material that can later be used in the reflection at the end of the session.

✦ **Introduce the objectives and the agenda.** We introduce the objectives and plan for the event with reference to the expectations of participants and negotiate any changes. In this process we clearly name expectations that:

✧ are already part of the agenda
✧ cannot be met, which are outside the scope of the session
✧ can be included but would require some redesigning. At the subsequent session we can return with a concrete proposal for discussion about how these can be met.

A well-thought-out introduction to the program is evidence of your preparation and can be part of establishing your credibility. It is also a mark of respect for the participants.

✦ **Introduce the theme of the workshop.** This step can be part of the introductory exercises or activities for getting started, which we outline in chapter three. We've also found it useful to include an activity that helps the group situate itself in relation to the theme or topic: to look at who we are and who we aren't and at how these factors condition our relationship to the topic.

✦ **Negotiate the logistics.** At any event there is always a number of logistical problems to get out of the way before anything else can be done, from establishing guidelines on smoking to negotiating times for beginning and ending sessions. Especially in residential situations – when people are meeting in places overnight and far from home – participants not used to the situation will be preoccupied with questions about meals, telephones, and sleeping arrangements. Clarifying these logistics helps reduce anxiety – something we have underestimated in the past.

In union courses, a Class Steward is elected with responsibility for all logistics and complaints. Reviewing and negotiating the workshop schedule also help clarify logistics. We particularly check when people need to leave at the end of the session, because we prefer to finish early with most people there rather than having people drift out in ones and twos. A "collective agreement" might be developed to cover ground rules about logistics.

✦ **Set the atmosphere.** One important message people should get in the first hour is that we want them to participate in and take ownership of the event. To help establish this atmosphere, we choose introductory activities that give everyone a chance to participate. Within those activities there is often an opportunity to move the furniture around so that people will begin to claim the space as their own. (See chapter four, "USING SPACE: THE POLITICS OF FURNITURE.") We often establish a process for our work together by putting forward our assumptions about the process and negotiating those with participants. We post a list of these assumptions and use them as a reference throughout the session.

DMI ARCHIVES

Our assumptions about a workshop: a sample list*

■ Everyone will help contribute to a safe/non-judgmental environment.
■ Much of the content will be coming from the participants.
■ Participants bring analysis/experience to the program.
■ Everyone will have a shared intolerance for all forms of oppression.
■ Participants will take responsibility for their own learning and interaction with other participants.
■ Everyone will participate fully in all sessions.
■ People will bring a sense of humour.
■ Everyone will set objectives for a three-hour workshop and design one activity.
■ There will be tolerance of differences in approaches and strategies.

Chapter three outlines some of the activities we use for getting started. We also use a summary checklist – and when we forget three or four items on this list we know later on why things didn't go as well as they could have.

A getting started checklist

■ introductions to each other
■ set the atmosphere, build the group
■ reflect on the social identity of the group in relation to the topic
■ identify participant expectations
■ introduce the theme of the workshop
■ introduce the objectives and the plan for the event, referring to the expectations of the participants
■ get people "there" mentally as well as physically
■ establish a process for the event with participants
■ clear up any logistical details (washrooms, lunch)
■ negotiate ground rules (smoking, meeting times)
■ give participants a chance to claim the space in the room

* Two of us prepared this list for a five-day workshop with the African National Congress in Lusaka in January 1990. We also included several assumptions about ourselves: 1) we know less than participants do about this social context; 2) the fact that we are White Canadian women has shaped our particular knowledge, experience, and perspectives; and 3) we bring a knowledge of the theory and practice of social change education and will contribute it as appropriate.

Getting out people's experience or knowledge of a theme

Starting with what people know – with their experience – provides an important statement to the participants. It says that we value what they know, that their experience is important. It also helps people recognize their own personal resources: how much they can learn from each other; how much they already know about a theme.

Feedback from many participants tells us that this beginning is also an important moment for starting to build a different kind of relationship between student and teacher. There is a sense of energy released in a session as we uncover the richness of experience and resources with a diverse group of people.

For the educator/facilitator this beginning also provides invaluable knowledge. It's a way of determining what people already know, so that you won't bore them with old information.

Besides these practical considerations, there are clear political implications in not putting people's knowledge and experience at the centre of the program and making them central to the opening session of any educational program. What messages do we convey through an education that feeds information to people, assuming they know nothing? Such practices come down again to supporting the dominant social belief in experts (usually those sanctioned by people in power). Instead of encouraging action, these practices encourage passivity. Both the content and the process of education are political.

We must admit that several educators, reflecting on their own experience, have taken issue with us on this point. They say, "But it is often the participants themselves who want to hear from the expert. They want us to give the input – and feel that talking about their experience is a waste of time." This response really isn't a surprise when you reflect on the two dominant educators in Canada: the schools and the mass media. In these two key outlets the knowledge that is valued comes from experts and not from experience, feelings, and intuition. An important task we have as educators for social change is to encourage people to value their own experience, to increase our collective self-confidence to act for change, including change in the process and/or content of the education program itself.

Most often, we find, participants embrace the chance to talk about their own experience. The resistance comes from educators: worried about what will happen if they give up control; afraid of "not having all the answers"; concerned about people coming to the "right" conclusions. As social change educators, if we only talk about people taking control and don't adapt truly democratic practices in our education programs, we are working against our own long-term goal of supporting people to empower themselves to transform society.

Tips on pulling out people's experience and knowledge

A reader of an early draft of this chapter made it to this point and said, "That's all very well, but how do we do this?" Chapter three provides part of the answer, with its outline of the activities we've found useful at this stage of our workshops. Here also are some of the points our experience has taught us to consider in pulling out people's experience.

✦ **what experience gets shared where and why.** Since their own experience is something people know a lot about, you need to carefully draw out the information from this experience that you want to work with later. For instance, if you generate more information than you will be able to process later on, people may feel frustrated or even negated because part of their material isn't used.

✦ **how much data you want to take up in the full group.** We may have people discuss three questions in small groups but ask them to report back on only one. Participants should know in advance that only one question will be shared with other groups.

✦ **the emotional impact of sharing experiences on the theme.** In a workshop with women educators working on the issue of woman abuse, we did not take sufficiently into account the fact that there would be abused women in the group who would need additional time and support to deal with their own pain. The emotional cost to a person will be directly related to his/her social identity and relationship to the theme of the session.

✦ **the social identities and mixture of the group.** In a session on racism, for example, it is crucial to consider the relationship of participant experience to the theme. If there is to be a mix of people of colour and White people, the dynamic this will produce must be taken into account in your design. For example, there is the threat to a person of colour of "voyeurism" by White participants who don't need to deal with the day-to-day lived reality of racism.

✦ **the ways in which participant experience relates to the topic.** In a workshop on the media, for example, the way in which participant experience relates to the theme will be very different for journalists or community people interested in media access. In a session that includes both groups, how can you create an opportunity for learning from each other? If only one group is present, how can your design include the other voices?

✦ **the kinds of questions you will ask.** We have found that coming up with the right questions is the single most important decision we make. The questions need to be few, clear, simple, and considered from all angles. There are other considerations as well, such as whether to have open or closed questions or to identify "generative" questions on a theme. *

* For more on questions, we suggest the article "How to use questions effectively," by Patrick Suessmuth in *Ideas for Training Managers and Supervisors* (La Jolla, California: University Associates, 1978).

53

Looking for patterns in our experience

Canadians do have the "freedom to choose" – from among, for instance, some fifteen different brands of washing detergent. The choice of course, is often an illusion, because a handful of companies put out the "different" brands and most if not all of the soap is more or less the same. But this illusion of a "freedom to choose" – with the focus on our individual rights and freedoms – creates a special challenge for educators working to build collective action for social change.

For us, the step of collectivizing experience, then, is very important. And for us one of the fundamentals of collectivizing experience in educational events is (perhaps ironically) to break down into small groups so voices have a chance to be heard. Then those voices are brought back in some form (through an appointed speaker or a dramatization, for instance) to the full group or plenary session, where we look for patterns in common.

After people have had an opportunity to talk about their experience and identify patterns, something we often hear is, "And I thought I was the only one." By finding patterns we recognize that many of our problems aren't ours alone and, just as important, aren't our "fault".

How can it be "just my fault" when other people say they've had similar experiences? When we identify patterns we also try to keep in mind the difference between what it means to have the same experience and what it means to have similarities in certain aspects of our experience because of different social identities.

In collectivizing knowledge or experience, we have the opportunity to learn from each other. Participants in a workshop or other event can also realize how much they know collectively, as a group.

Take a quick look at the graphic below. How many squares are there?*

Now ask some other people near you to look at the design. How many squares do they see? How many do you see when you work together? There are supposed to be thirty-one squares. Our group could only find thirty (1x16, 4x9, 9x4, 16x1) – if you find the other one, please let us know.

You might want to use this exercise in your organization to make the point that collectivizing knowledge and experience is worthwhile.

---

* University Associates, California. Used in adapted form in union education, including *Steelworker Training Manual for Local Officers*, Toronto, 1984.

Tips on collectivizing experience and knowledge

✦ **Don't suppress difference.** In focusing on the patterns in experience it is important to acknowledge and engage difference. One useful question is: What are the similarities and the differences in your experiences? For example, men (non-harassers) and women see the prevalence of sexual harassment in the workplace in totally different ways.

✦ **Arrange the process to ensure that everyone has a voice.** When you have small groups reporting back to a large plenary, how often have you seen a first group using up all the time and covering all the points,so the others are left feeling frustrated and disappointed? To avoid this, we sometimes ask people to present one point only, so we can move along and make sure that the last person or group will not only have time but also still have something to add.

✦ **Ensure that the plenary isn't a repeat.** It's frustrating for participants if the plenary simply repeats what took place in the small groups. So we have to consider how the collectivizing of the experience will move the discussion forward (raise a new point, expand on an important issue). You might ask groups to identify points of energy or tension as the focus for deeper plenary discussion. (See chapter three, "STEPS OR MOMENTS IN AN ACTIVITY," for different ways of reporting back from small groups.)

✦ **Consider the range of organizational roles among participants.** The degree of variety among the people you're working with will influence how much time you need to take things up. For instance, in a workshop with a whole organization where you have a mix of program staff, management, and board, you will need longer than if you were working with only one of these groups.

✦ **Don't try to pursue everything in depth.** We always have to select – that's why establishing clear objectives is so important. Focus on one or two central ideas and let the rest just flow on past or flag them for another time and place. One caution: it is possible for a key point that wasn't considered in the objectives to emerge in the process. Check with the group to see if they want to refocus the session or pursue the original design.

✦ **Have participants look critically at their experience.** There are some questions that help to do this. Are there any surprises? Insights? Do you see any patterns? How do your (individual) experiences compare with the general patterns we seem to be seeing? What are the similarities and differences in the presentations?

Adding theory / new information

One of the misconceptions about popular education or social change education is that all of the information has to come from the participants themselves. On the contrary: we feel it is important not to limit people to the information and experience they have in the room. Although we want to validate participant experience and knowledge, we do not want to romanticize it.

But it is true that for social change educators whose task is to empower people, how we add new information takes on political importance. Our process must affirm what people already know while suggesting new questions and frameworks for deepening understanding. For example, in doing workshops with educators we encourage the participants to share from their own experience what helps and hinders their learning. After collectivizing that material we briefly introduce the principles of adult and social change education and provide theory on how people learn. (This is where the "learning heads" introduced earlier come in.) But we make a point of showing participants how they had identified most of those principles and theories in their own learning. Now, we hope, their own learning has been put forward in a framework to which future experience and information can be attached.

Adding new material can also be an opportunity to connect to other, outside struggles and issues. For example, in a workshop with food industry workers in Canada we looked at building alliances with other sectors in their industry. After we spent some time considering the successes and failures of the participants' past experience in alliance building in Canada, we introduced a case study of the Guatemalan Coca Cola workers. As we looked for similarities and differences between the two cases, some additional strategies suggested themselves for possible use by their unions. The workshop also built solidarity – ending with a telegram of support from participants to those on strike in Guatemala City.

Participants often have specialized knowledge that we can draw upon in the workshops; and/or we can bring in outside resource people and resources. In addition to deliberate presentations, we shape the information that is generated by how we structure the sharing of knowledge and experience among participants, by the questions we pose, by the issues we take up, by the anecdotes we add to participant comments, and by using case studies and other exercises.

Nor does new input have to be limited to the session itself. It's always good to come up with a collective list of reading materials or human resources for future consultation; we often use a flip-chart for this purpose.

THE LEARNING HEADS

hear only

see only

hear and see

hear, see and talk

hear, see, talk, do

% we retain   20%   30%   50%   70%   90%

EDUCATING FOR A CHANGE

Tips on adding theory/new information

✦ **participant energy level and the time of day.** As a rule of thumb, we try not to make presentations just after lunch. When we see from body language and drooping eyes that energy is sagging, we add energizers. A few of our favourites are included with the activities in chapter three.

✦ **how people learn.** Keeping in mind our learning heads, in adding new information we try to use as many of the senses as possible for greatest retention.

✦ **organizational culture.** We need to be sensitive to organizational culture as we introduce new content. How large trade unions make decisions or share information is very different from the way small community resource centres do. So when we add new information we consider what will be most effective in the particular organizational context. Print? Film? An oral presentation? A play?

✦ **what resources are available.** This comes back to advance planning: we need to do research before the event to see whether there are resource people, audio-visuals, or other resources we should consider using.

✦ **literacy levels of participants.** This consideration will help determine what if any of the resources on the topic are appropriate to your situation.

✦ **the question of voice.** It is crucial to critically preview any audio-visual resource before we use it with special attention to the issue of voice: what is the racial, ethnic, and class makeup of the resource and the perspective of its message? Our bibliography here lists several resources that help identify the questions we should all be asking about the audio-visuals we use. But it's also possible to use less-than-perfect materials critically and involve participants in raising questions of voice.

✦ **how to relate new content to what participants already know about the topic.** To aid understanding, we need to be clear about how the new information or theory relates to what we already know. One way to do this is to build in a continual review of new input in light of experience.

ALOK MUKHERJEE

Practising skills, forming strategies, and planning for action

After sharing and analysing experiences and deepening understanding through the input of new information and theory, participants are usually ready to act on what they've learned.

As we've seen with the learning heads, most learning occurs when people try on what they've learned – when they do something with it. So one thing we want to ensure is that participants have a chance to practise their skills. It's like public-speaking courses that use video to give participants a chance to practise in front of a video camera, with co-participants as their audience.

We also want to make sure that there is time to form strategies and plan for action. It is in this commitment – to take action – that social change education radically departs from mainstream adult education.

Our school system poses education as exposure to ideas – learning "all sides" of a question. Individual students, presumably, are left to make up their own minds about what to think. When teachers discuss action they tend to do so in the abstract and as a personal (or private) matter for their students. They limit action to activities that are not too "political".

While our task as social change educators is not to define for people how they should act, our programs assume that change comes about because people take action, collectively as well as individually. One of our goals is to strengthen organizations – and organizing skills. We are involved in education for action.

Tips on practising skills

✦ **Consider the risk involved in "performing" before your peers.** When, for instance, participants in an event are video-taped in front of the others, most of them tend to get very anxious. They all want to do well but are sure they'll mess up. So we need to take steps to make sure everyone feels safe in this kind of situation. Something that has worked well for us is to have participants develop guidelines for giving feedback to each other. This process is described in more detail in chapter four, "GIVING AND GETTING FEEDBACK."

✦ **Give participants control over any product.** For example, when we make videotapes in a workshop, we give the participants a copy of their presentations and feedback to keep. If we want to use any aspect of it in other contexts, we negotiate its use with the person(s) involved.

✦ **Build in adequate preparation time.** The workshop design needs to allow people enough time to prepare to practise their new skills in front of their colleagues. Without adequate preparation, the anxiety level increases and people are more likely not to do well.

✦ **Design time both to practise and to discuss the experience.** Adequate discussion time is especially important for participants who are not happy with their "performance". But for all participants there is a great deal of learning in the reactions of their peers, as well as in the unravelling of their own experience during the practice exercise. If the practising of skills runs overtime, which it often does, be sure that everyone gets time to practise and that the last few people aren't rushed. This means that you need to consider beforehand what you are willing to drop from the program.

58

**Tips on forming
strategies and
planning for action**

✦ **Consider the organizational context.** What are the possibilities for action and application within the organization(s) represented by the participants? If possible, clarify this information in advance with the planning committee.

✦ **Find out where and with whom people will be exerting influence.** In action planning, we often consider the use of caucuses: that is, whether there is merit in dividing participants according to their location within the organization. For example, in a union session we might have the stewards in one group and the local union officers in another.

✦ **Consider both collective and individual action.** We strongly encourage collective action, allocating most of the discussion time to group strategies. It's also important to give participants a chance to focus on their individual roles and responsibilities in follow-up action. One tool we've used is the "letter to yourself" at the end of a session. Participants write a letter to themselves, outlining what they want to have accomplished by the time the letter is mailed to them in the future (the date is predetermined). The facilitator collects the sealed letters and mails them as follow-up on the predetermined date. A collective letter, produced as a summary of proposed actions and posted in the workplace, can also be a powerful reference.

✦ **Leave time to identify the next steps for whatever action is called for.** Before people leave the session, we usually identify some "next steps" – who will do what and when. In some cases there is also a need to identify a co-ordinating group or follow-up committee.

✦ **Identify how you will evaluate the proposed action.** How will you know if you have been successful? When and how will you critically review the action and see what new strategies are called for?

DEBORAH BARNDT

Reflection and evaluation

As social change educators, we also want to find ways to open up our work to constructive criticism.

We used to only do evaluations at the end of the event, asking questions like: Did we accomplish what we set out to do? Did the people who came meet their objectives? One problem we've faced, though, is that participants tend to be polite at the end of a session whereas in the middle they are more likely to be frank because their input could affect their own learning.

Increasingly we realized that to be effective we needed information from participants during an event about both the content and the process so that we could make the necessary changes as we went along. We ask some of these questions:

✧ What are you learning? How are you feeling?
✧ How is the content useful? What else do you need?
✧ Who has participated/who hasn't? Why?
✧ How is the pacing? Too fast or too slow?
✧ How is the balance between new and familiar content?
✧ How is the language level? What has been clear/unclear?

So we began to build in evaluation as a reflection on the process, throughout the event. That's why we place "reflection" in the middle of the spiral. One activity we use – which we call "the Fly on the Ceiling" – involves participants stopping each day to reflect on what they've been through. This gives all of us an opportunity to look back and ask ourselves: What did we do? What did we learn or feel? What can we use or adapt for our own work?

We also use "Process Observer Reports": each day two participants take responsibility for collecting information from the others and for delivering a verbal report on the process at the beginning of the next session.

We describe these activities, along with others, in greater detail in the next chapter. We find that not only does ongoing reflection give us information we can use to modify the design as we go along, but it also helps participants take greater ownership of the process. Feedback indicates that when the facilitators are open to the frank, honest critique of participants, we help build more equal relations among everyone.

Some educators worry that this built-in repeated reflection takes up too much time. But, for our part, we made an extremely liberating discovery we'd like to share with you: you don't have to cover all of the items on your agenda. As social change educators we are trying to empower people for action, and sometimes that means encountering resistance. If we cram the session so full that every participant voice that is raised seems to be a delay, what does that say about the importance we attach to the views of participants?

We have found that the element of time can be used as a mask for underlying political values or choices. Participants will most likely read "We don't have enough time for that" as "This doesn't matter" or "I don't want to do it".

We think it's important to build in time for people to take control of the education process, to negotiate real changes in the agenda, and to resist overload.

Sometimes it is necessary to have a formal evaluation at the end of the event, for political reasons (funders demand it) or maybe because it was a pilot program and you require the information. End-of-session evaluations can also become an integral and critical part of the learning process – building on ideas that came up earlier and are just beginning to be digested.

Even when there is no need for a final evaluation, there is a need for wrapping up, for closure. Some of this need has to do with human stuff, like goodbyes. Some of it has to do with follow-up, with being sure that everyone is clear on who should do what. The next chapter includes some of the activities we've used for end-of-session reflection.

RICK ARNOLD

BARB THOMAS

Tips on building in reflection

✦ **time for redesigning.** When they build in the space for participant critique and suggestions, facilitators also require time to take that information into account and redesign the agenda as they go along. They may have to miss lunch, stay up late, or, preferably, build meeting times into the agenda during periods when participants have free time. We also ask participants to put forth any major proposals for change as early as possible, or we can't be responsible for the failure to address them.

✦ **the length of the session.** There is both more need – and more time – for reflection during a long event than during a short one. But even in a shorter session, a one-day workshop for instance, we build in a mid-point check on how things are going.

✦ **where to cut your agenda.** Most of us suffer from the tendency to overdesign – to pack too much into an irresistible agenda. In our experience, cutting in the middle is always best. Keep the opening and closing. You need to ensure that you don't cut out the time you need at the beginning to lay the group foundation for good working relations, or the time at the end for the action discussion.

This is not a call for activism over analysis. Rather, we recognize the importance of moving through all of the moments on the spiral and of making sure we don't drop off planning action due to lack of time.

✦ **what you want feedback on.** The specific points for reflection change during an event. While the earlier part tends to focus on more general questions (what was useful/not useful), later on the focus may fix on one specific problem. For example, in one workshop for community educators we had a day that was too full, so that participants were exhausted at the end. The reflection focused on this problem: what it felt like, how it happened, and how it could be avoided.

✦ **time for discussion.** In designing a program we try to include time for people to think individually or in pairs about the questions posed, and for general discussion. It's especially important to arrange time for general discussion when there have been problems in the process of working together that the group needs to address, or when a group needs to develop a collective commitment to a common action plan.

✦ **making visible participant input.** Using a flip-chart, we write up the objectives and agenda for each day and review the whole program during the first session. Based on continuing participant input, we revise the agenda and note any changes in a different colour with a marker pen. In longer courses we review the revised agenda for each day at the beginning of the morning, noting how we have taken participant suggestions into account.

A twist in the spiral Now that you're ready to try out the spiral design model, we have one more twist for you. If we did a drawing of many of our events, this is how they might end up looking:

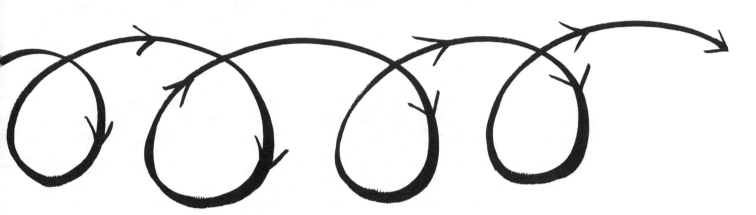

The sketch may look like a slinky toy, but its purpose is to illustrate that the model is not fixed or linear. In any one session you may travel through the phases of the model several times. Another variation might look like this:

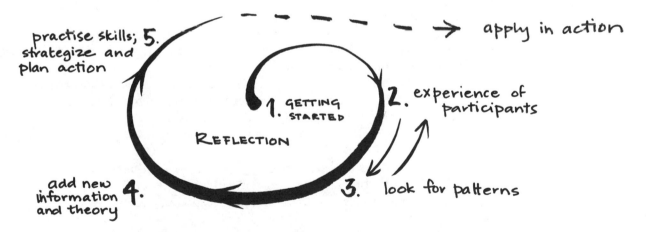

In this one the arrows move back and forth between the stages of sharing experience and of finding patterns. In this workshop people shared their experience and explored patterns on two aspects of the theme before moving on to add new information and theory.

For us the importance of the spiral model is the way it helps us to think through the design – beginning with what people know, with their experience, before moving on to new information and theory and ending with action, where they use the new learning to help contribute in some way to the process of social change.

63

Documenting the process

"Our event was a great success!! Too bad no one thought of keeping notes or taking photos. I guess it will have to live on with the rest of our oral tradition."

Documenting our work is a political responsibility. We took the first step towards doing it when we began to record and keep our own design outlines on paper. The second step was raising the issue of documentation of the event for participants in the planning process.

Documenting the design

In the past some of us have taken pride in our capacity to "wing it" and have been effective solo performers. But if our goal is to build stronger collective organizations, the "winging it" style has serious drawbacks. Documenting an event is one way of including, of making explicit and available, what may otherwise appear to be our individual, personal talents.

Before we began recording and keeping our designs we couldn't draw from our past work in a systematic way. We also had difficulty sharing that work, both with other educators and with the participants. So we began to write down our designs, and now we use a "design sheet" as a way to record our intended designs and leave room for revisions as we go along.

We often hand these design sheets out to participants at the end of the event, especially to educators who may want to adapt a design for their own use. For us this work is all part of demystifying the process of educational leadership. This demystification is in turn an integral part of the democratic process.

Documenting an event

A video? A photostory? A written report? The nature of the documentation depends on the objectives of the event, on who will use the report and how, and on the equipment and resources available.

Increasingly we find that participants want their work returned to them, preferably during the event. So in longer sessions we put the material generated in each session onto a flip-chart and then into the computer. If we have access to duplicating facilities we can make copies available for participants the following day.

Participants can also share in the process of documentation. In one workshop a production subgroup produced a booklet of the event and had it photocopied for all participants in time for the closing ceremony.

DEBORAH BARNDT

Design Sheet

Name of Workshop _____

Participants

Objectives
1.
2.
3.
4.

Time	Activity/Details of the process	Materials needed	Person Responsible

EDUCATING FOR A CHANGE

**Tips on building in
documentation**

✦ Assume your experience is valuable to someone else.

✦ Raise the issue of documentation in the planning process.

✦ Decide in advance who will use the information, and how.

✦ Name particular persons and groups who may be interested in the report.

✦ Take the resources available (financial, material, human) into account.

✦ Based on the above decisions decide on format (print, video, photos, manual, or descriptive), when to produce the document (during or after the workshop), and what its basic structure or content will include.

✦ Decide who will be responsible for documentation during the session and for pulling the material together following the event.

✦ Make a realistic estimate of the time needed to turn the raw material into a usable document.

✦ Identify resources needed (financial, material, human).

Documentation is one of the ways we, as educators, can make sure we follow our own model and apply in action what we've learned in the workshop.

BARB THOMAS

A DESIGNING
CHECKLIST

In training workshops we've done, one exercise we've often used is to have people reflect on what helps them learn and what hinders them. After talking about these experiences, participants are asked to review the material generated and come up with a checklist of what makes for effective workshop planning and design.

We drew on the work of those participants earlier in this chapter when we outlined a checklist for planning. Here we offer a summary checklist for effective design, which once again draws on the expertise of workshop participants.

We've left room for you to add any points we've missed.

A checklist for effective design

■ Have a planning committee of participants to help in the design

■ Take into account what you know about the participants

■ Visit the site and take the physical space into account in the design

■ State your own assumptions in advance

■ Take into account the organizational and broader societal context for the event

■ Be clear about what kinds of events/actions have come before and will follow this session

■ Anticipate potential problems and how they might be handled

■ Have clear, stated objectives that follow the spiral design circle

■ Have a clear, written agenda, which fits the time available

■ Have a mix of activities that encourage participation and take into account the background of participants

■ Build in ways for participants to gradually take more control of the process

■ Know how people will be broken down into groups and how the groups will report back

■ Plan for breaks, energizers, humour

■ Build in evaluation during and after the event

■ Identify clear responsibility for follow-up

■ Have a clear plan for documenting the process for participants

■ Review your plan and cut it down; you probably have too much

■

■

■

■

3

Shaping Our Tools:
Developing and Using Activities

6 LOOKING FORWARD:
Implications for our work
in the 1990's

5 LOOKING BACK:
Issues emerging from our practice

3 SHAPING OUR TOOLS
Developing and
Using Activities

2 WORKING BY DESIGN:
Putting together a program

4 WORKING ON OUR FEET:
The practice of democratic
facilitation

1 THIS IS OUR CHANCE:
Educating Strategically

As you've worked through this book so far, there may have been a lingering question echoing in the back of your mind: "This is fine – but I have an event to plan for next week. How can I get started, get out people's experience, find the patterns, add new theory and information, practise skills, make strategies, and plan for action, and evaluate? Give me some examples."

In this chapter we begin answering this question by outlining some of the activities we've used at the various stages of the spiral design model.

First we want to clarify what we mean by "an activity". Here's why....

We were in the second day of a five-day program with community educators. We had introduced the spiral design model, made some progress with the worksheet on objectives, and were moving into designing a piece of an educational event. One of the facilitators went to the flip-chart and asked: "What are the steps in any activity?"

There was silence until someone said, "Getting out experience" and someone else said, "Planning". The facilitator, a little flustered, began to write down what soon became a jumbled list of items.

*After a few minutes of this it became clear that we had made an incorrect assumption: the term "activity" was **not** commonly understood by everyone.*

ACTIVITIES AND HOW TO CHOOSE THEM

What is an activity?

For us, an "activity" is a tool we use to meet an objective in an educational event.

We divide activities into three types:

◇ presentations
◇ guided discussions
◇ structured activities

Many people continue to be most comfortable with the **presentation,** either verbal or audio-visual. The **guided discussion** requires skill in ensuring broad participation and finding the right questions. The **structured activity** (role-playing for example) can be the most dynamic activity but many educators see it as having the highest risk factor.

In the following pages we are referring only to structured activity. But in fact a mix of all three kinds of activities is often what's needed to make sure your program relates to the learning styles of all the participants.

Structured activities most often involve breaking down a body of participants (ideally anywhere from fifteen to twenty-five people) into smaller groups. Whatever the mode of activity (role-play, drama, doing drawings, or just straight discussion), we usually ask participants to consider several questions prepared in the design phase.

Steps or moments in an activity

One way to begin is to dissect an activity into its component parts.

1. Introduction: explaining the activity

✦ **Give the background to the activity and its objective.** We usually begin by explaining to participants why we are asking them to do the activity. In these opening remarks we sometimes include a little history or background if appropriate, or we try to allay any possible fears. For example, in the introduction to drama or role-play we emphasize that there are no acting awards given and that for those who don't want to take a leading role there is always a bit-part – a palm tree, perhaps.

We've also found that we need to be comfortable with the activity if we are to help others feel comfortable doing it. And when we introduce an activity we can afford to wander a little at the beginning, but by the end of the introduction we need to be very precise about the instructions.

✦ **Explain the guidelines, the task, and the time available.** Participants need to know exactly what they are being asked to do. We often write the task – which often involves considering a list of questions related to the topic – on a flip-chart so everyone can see it.

If people will be working in different rooms, or if the task is complicated, we hand out a tasksheet to each person. The tasksheet includes the question to be discussed/worked at; how the work is to be recorded; what should be reported back to the full group; how much time people have. (There's a sample tasksheet in the "Nightmares" section of this chapter.) Check with the group to make sure members understand the task and are willing to engage in it. Leave room for questions.

✦ **Hand out materials; tell people how to divide into groups and where to go.** If there are handouts or other materials these need to be identified and a process suggested for getting them to each group. Before the activity starts you may also have to divide people into small groups. It's good to assign groups ahead of time to ensure a mix of different experiences. (For a guideline, you may want to refer to the power flower in chapter one as a checklist of considerations.)

In every session there will also be informal, pre-existing cliques. So when people break into small groups we need to take these cliques into account, either to encourage people to mix or to take advantage of existing relationships.

For a longer program we like to have two or three ways to divide people into groups. Don't forget that you'll need to be clear about where each group can work, but this information is better given after people are divided into groups. Otherwise they often don't remember where to go.

Ideas for dividing people into groups

■ **number off by the number of groups you need.** So for a session of twenty people where you want to form four small groups, participants would number off from one to four. Have people group afterwards by number into the four groups.

■ **by symbols.** Prepare pieces of paper with as many different symbols as you need groups. If you want to form four groups of five people you might have five triangles, squares, circles, and rectangles. Each person picks a symbol and finds others with the same symbol.

■ **self-selection.** When you want people to divide into groups according to their interest in a topic or theme, you can post the topics in different places on the wall around the room. Ask participants to "vote with their feet" by going to the topic that most interests them. If there are too many people for any given theme, you can subdivide the group. If there is no interest in a given topic, it doesn't get discussed.

■ **by sound.** This is useful for later in a longer program after people have got to know one another and won't feel self-conscious. It uses the same process as the symbol method, although this time each person gets a piece of paper describing a sound. Participants find their group by moving around the room, making the sound. To make it even more interesting people can do the activity with their eyes closed. We use animal sounds, machine sounds, baby sounds – use your imagination, have fun!

■ **pre-formed groups.** Sometimes you need to have a particular mix of people for specific purposes; so you list the group members and where they will be working on a flip-chart and post them. Preparing the list in advance can save time and avoid confusion during the session.

73

2. Preparing the activity

✦ When participants are working at something – preparing a role play, engaging in a discussion to draw together ideas or prepare a report – we, as facilitators, usually do not participate in the activity because our presence can impede or distract the group's own work. In these situations the role of the facilitator is to be a resource person, to clarify instructions, and to help out any group having difficulties. We also have to watch the clock.

3. Presenting and discussing the activity

✦ Small groups report back to the larger group. Most educators (and participants) have experienced more than their share of boring plenaries. So it's important to plan carefully just how to get the most out of the larger group discussion: to decide what needs to be shared and how.

Ways of reporting back from small groups

- **different questions from each group.** Each group reports back on a different question. All the questions are covered once.
- **only one question reported back.** Groups report back on only one of the questions discussed (the key question). Notes on other questions might be posted so other groups can take a look at them during a break.
- **different forms of report back.** Each group can be asked to use a different form of report back (visual, dramatic, verbal, song etc.) or can choose the form the members feel most comfortable with.
- **simultaneous plenaries.** We use this method when small groups have prepared skits or dramatic presentations and the group as a whole is too large for everyone to see all of the presentations. We break the main body of participants into as many large groups as we need, with one facilitator and three to four presentations in each. All of these mini-plenaries can take place at the same time.
- **gallery review.** Each group posts its material and participants walk around this instant gallery to see what others have done. A representative of each group should remain with that group's work to help answer questions from other participants. You can also leave space in the group's charts for comments or questions from the other participants.

■ **a common format.** About fifteen or twenty minutes before the end of the small-group discussion period, you ask each group to focus on its report back and to synthesize the discussion. You can provide a sample format:

The main points we discussed were (no more than 3)
1.
2.
3.
and we concluded that _____
_____
we recommend _____
_____
One of the most interesting/exciting points we discussed
and would like to share with the plenary _____
_____

It helps to emphasize to participants that this format is not to be taken as a formula to be strictly followed.*

■ **no report back.** Sometimes, due to time constraints or the nature of the discussion, it is not possible or necessary to hear back from the small groups – although, in our experience, this does not happen very often. In a plenary it's also possible to ask for comments from the floor on the key points or issues raised.

■ **Pulling out the experience.** After the small groups return to the plenary, the next step involves asking questions about the small-group work that will make sure participants describe the experience and identify patterns.

Questions for this step might be: What are your findings? What are your key learnings or insights?

■ **Looking for patterns/analysis.** This is the meat of any activity. After all the reports have been completed, you can ask a number of questions about what's been reported: What are the similarities and the differences? What helped or hindered? Who benefited? Who lost? What are the key shared concerns? What issues should we focus our discussion on now?

■ **Add new content/theory.** After the analysis of participant experience we can introduce new content or theory, either through a brief facilitator presentation or a handout.

■ **Synthesis.** The final step in any activity is the summary or synthesis of the most important points that emerged in the discussion. Participants and facilitators can work together to name key issues in summary form.

---

* Thanks to Lily Mah-Sen, who contributed this idea.

Steps or moments in an activity

1. Introduction: explaining the activity
■ explain the objectives of the activity
■ give the history/background of the activity if appropriate
■ explain the task and the time available, checking for clarity and consent
■ identify and distribute materials/handouts if any
■ groupings – how to divide and where to go

2. Preparing the activity
■ participants work at something, often in groups (preparation)
■ facilitator is available as a resource or to clarify
■ facilitator monitors time

3. Presenting and discussing the activity
■ if in small groups, come back to larger group
■ pull out the experience
■ look for patterns/analysis
■ add new content/theory
■ synthesis

Deciding on an activity

The activities we draw on are limited only by our ability to create and re-create them. It's possible to borrow and adapt activities from many different sources. For instance, the "liberal" education stance, with its strength in the development of participatory activities, offers teambuilding and communications activities that we've found particularly adaptable for more social or political purposes.

For instance, an activity developed by University Associates, California, a training centre in the liberal tradition, stresses the importance of visual communication. One participant describes what's in a map, without the aid of visuals, and other participants try to draw the map from what they hear. A DMI member adapted the same activity for a strike course. He had one trade unionist in a group describe a plant layout and where picket lines should go; and got the other members to do a drawing of what they heard.

The facilitator used the same process and made the same point about the importance of visual communication. But he also used the tool to meet an organizing objective – to familiarize people with the picket lines.

The problem for many of us becomes how to decide what you need for a specific group at a specific time to meet a specific objective. The activities you use also need to take into account the local context and the availability of technology and resources. This is where it helps to have some of the participants or group representatives involved in the planning.

Participants in past workshops have contributed to this checklist of things to consider.

A checklist for developing appropriate activities

Consider

- the local context
- the number of participants
- who the participants are: their cultural background, sector, social class, race, gender, traditions
- the comfort level: will participants feel uncomfortable doing the activity at this stage in the event?
- objectives
- the design: at what point in the workshop should you do this activity? Should you use it to draw out participant experience, analyse a topic, add new information, or make an action plan?
- the time of day
- the time you have available
- language/level and literacy
- space, logistics
- the materials and technology available/required
- theme/subject matter
- the resources available to you
- participant experience, how much they know about the theme
- organizational context (timing, who is involved)
- your nightmares, and potential resistance to the activity

But we've found that there is another way in which people come at this question of activities. Educators may have experienced or read about a particular activity that they want to use. Is it suitable for the specific situation? An activity grid can help answer that question. The grid does not pretend to include all possibilities. Again, we are emphasizing structured activities because most of the questions we get refer to that category.

OBJECTIVES

Objectives	Paired Interview	Role Play: Prepared Script	Role Play: Participant Created ①	Skits	Stop Drama ②	Sculpture	Collage	Drawing	Songwriting	Video Participant Work	Presentation: Verbal ③	Presentation: Audio Visual	Small Group Tasks	Buzz Groups ④	Warmup Exercises ⑤	Case Studies	Storytelling	Written Handouts	Brainstorming	Line Ups ⑥	Flip Chart Processing	Stopping the Process	Questionnaire	Ads	Photostories		
1. Get to know each other	X												X	X	X		X			X					X		
2. Introduce a theme		X		X							X						X		X								
3. Get out expectations													X	X						X	X		X				
4. Get out participant knowledge/experience			X	X			X	X	X				X				X				X				X		
5. Find patterns in experience							X	X	X				X								X				X		
6. Analyze a theme		X				X					X		X											X	X		
7. Add new information/theory		X									X	X				X	X	X			X						
8. Practise skills			X		X					X			X			X											
9. Stategize & plan for action			X		X	X							X	X		X			X		X						
10. Reflect on process/evaluate	X												X	X							X		X		X		
11. Open and heal tensions					X															X		X					
12. Deal with sluggishness				X											X												
13. Have fun			X	X			X	X							X									X	X		
14. Build personal confidence among quiet participants	X									X			X	X													
15. Synthesize main points						X			X		X	X						X			X			X	X		
16. Introduce perspectives/voices not in the room		X					X					X				X	X	X							X		

① see "Nightmares" pg 86 ② for example see pg100 ③ There are many kinds of presentations: single speaker, panel etc.
④ quickly formed small groups to share ideas within a limited timeframe ⑤ for example pg 81,83,109,110
⑥ for example see pg 102

Reshaping an activity

Just as we have done with activities found here and there, we encourage you to plagiarize, reshape, and adapt our favourite activities to meet the needs of your own participants, themes, and objectives. We also hope that you will tell us about your new creations – so we can steal back from you as well.

We begin with a cautionary note. Using an activity is a bit like singing a folk song: we never use an activity exactly the same way twice. Each time we do a session with a different group of people – or even with the same group, but on a different theme or at a different moment in its organizational history – we rework the activity.

For example, when we work in landlocked areas, we remodel an introductory activity called "lifeboats" into one called "buses". You need to bring your own sense of the group and your own creative energy to this task of adapting – and that will make it more successful.

We've outlined the activities on separate pages to help make photocopying easier. And we've grouped them according to the stages of our spiral design model. There is also one category here that was not part of the spiral model: "Activities for energizing facilitators and participants". These are exercises we use during the session when energy is low, which often happens in mid-afternoon or when there has been too much of one kind of activity.

There are lots of other sources of activities you can consult, and we've included some of these in the bibliography. We have identified the source of each activity to the best of our knowledge: our apologies if we are unaware of having adapted someone else's work, and please do let us know so we can credit the original creators.

RICK ARNOLD

GETTING
STARTED

Buses or lifeboats: an introductory exercise

Why use it?
- to begin to get to know each other
- to have fun and relax
- to get a social X-ray of all of us as a group

Time it takes
- 15-30 minutes

What you need
- a large space, clear of furniture

How it's done
1. We ask everyone to stand up and come to the space chosen for the exercise.
2. We explain the objective. We usually mention that this activity is not intended to give people an in-depth introduction to each other; but it may introduce issues we will want to pursue later in greater depth.
3. We give the directions, with a short introduction appropriate to the group. We say, for example, "There's a social evening on Saturday in the city, and we will all have to travel by bus. So we thought we'd begin with some practice getting into the same bus – given that we come from so many different sectors and regions."
4. We explain they'll be asked to form buses in different ways. For example, "The men in one bus and the women in another". Or, "Get into buses by the region you live in." We usually ask people to make sure they move close together in the bus so they don't fall off.

    We say that no one can be in a bus by herself or himself, so if they have any trouble they should pick the most appropriate bus. For example, if we form buses by provinces and there's only one person from Manitoba, that person might want to join those from the closest province to form a larger (perhaps regional) bus.
5. We name the buses according to important features of the particular group (asking participants to form buses by where they were born, where they live, sector, organization, decade they were born, gender, number of children), making the buses appropriate to the group and the theme of the workshop.
6. We ask people in one or more buses to tell each other their names, organizations. We may also ask groups to tackle a specific task or question, such as "What are your hopes for this workshop?"
7. To avoid the process dragging, we try not to have too many buses and to minimize the time that people have to stay talking on their feet in each bus.
8. We summarize what we've learned about the group from this activity and note any specific questions the activity has raised.

Variations
- Arnold, Barndt, Burke, *A New Weave*, "Lifeboats", pp.17-19.

Source
- The Doris Marshall Institute (DMI).

Paired interviews

Why use it?
■ to get to know each other
■ to identify resources available within the group
■ to give each person an opportunity to make a presentation in front of the group

Time it takes
■ 1-2 hours

What you need
■ interview sheet handouts
■ pencils

How it's done
1. Ask the group to brainstorm a list of things they would like to know about each other. Post these questions on the flip-chart for everybody's reference.
2. Ask each person to pair up with someone else they don't already know (or don't know well). Using the questions as a guide, the two partners interview each other. Each partner records information about the other one on the interview sheet. (This task takes ten to fifteen minutes).
3. Participants introduce their partners to the group, using their interview sheets and keeping the introductions as brief as possible. This process can take some time, so in larger sessions it might be broken up over the course of the first day.
4. The facilitator collects the interview sheets. If resources exist, a master is prepared and duplicated for everyone before the end of the workshop.

Variation
■ The facilitator prepares an interview sheet ahead of time with questions related to the background of the workshop and with contact information.

Source
■ There are many different kinds of paired interviews. This version is thanks to Jeff Piker, Kingston, Ontario.

82

Starter puzzle

Why use it? ■ to get people to introduce themselves
■ to share expectations for the event

Time it takes ■ 10-30 minutes

What you need ■ photocopies of pictures related to the theme of the workshop, cut into 3-4 pieces so they form a kind of puzzle
■ a hat or basket for passing the pictures around

How it's done 1. Before the workshop we write questions for discussion on the back of the pictures. For example:
■ Tell the group who you are and where you work.
■ Tell us what you think the picture is portraying.
■ Tell us what you want to share, or what you want to learn in this session.
2. To begin, we ask each participant to choose one piece of the puzzle from a hat or basket.
3. We ask participants to search out the others who have the rest of their puzzle; they all put their pieces together and discuss the questions on the back.
4. We ask these small groups to write up the answers to the last question and post them on the wall – or share them with the other groups, depending on the time available and the number of participants.

Source ■ The Centre for Adult and Continuing Education (CACE), University of Western Cape, South Africa.

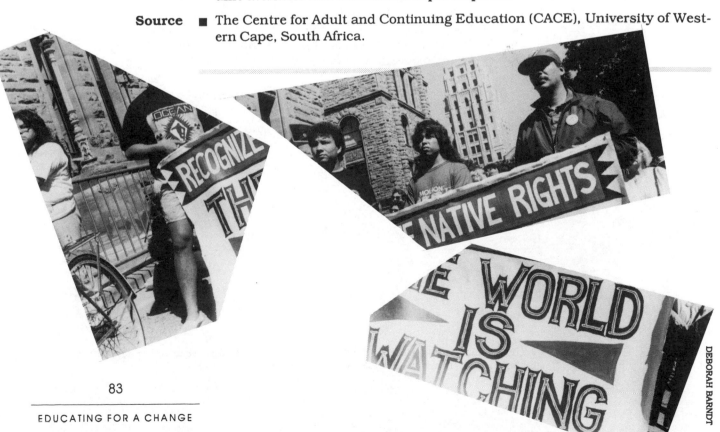

DEBORAH BARNDT

Three paired skirmish and round robin

Why use it?
- to get to know each other
- to share expectations for the workshop

Time it takes
- 15 minutes for skirmish
- 30-45 minutes for round robin

What you need
- flip-chart and markers
- questions written on a piece of flip-chart paper
- masking tape

How it's done
1. We write three questions on the flip-chart, and then tape the bottom end of the chart onto the top so that participants can't see the questions and we can roll the paper down one question at a time. Some sample questions:
   - What did you have to do to get here today?
   - What comes to your mind when you hear the term "popular education"?
   - What do you want to get out of this workshop?*
2. We ask people to find a partner – the person they know least well. When everyone has a partner we lower the paper so the first question becomes visible, and we explain the task: "Talk to your partner for five minutes about the question. When you hear me clap, change partners – find someone else you don't know very well – and I'll give you another question. You won't have to report back this question to the full group."
3. After three to five minutes, we clap (or sometimes shout) and again have people change partners. We do this once more. Before beginning the discussion of the third question we tell people that they'll have to report this answer back to the full group.
4. In the full group we do a round robin, so that everyone has a chance to say what they want to get out of the workshop. We usually write this information down on the flip-chart beside the person's name. We save the flip-chart papers to use in the evaluation at the end.

Variation
- You can adapt the activity using other questions – or for other objectives.

Source
- DMI.

---

* These questions assume that participants have already introduced each other using an exercise such as Buses. If this is the first exercise you would need to add introductions.

DRAWING OUT
KNOWLEDGE
AND
EXPERIENCE
AND LOOKING
FOR PATTERNS

Helps/hinders

Why use it?
- to identify key forces/elements that our organizations are up against and the main allies in our struggles

Time it takes
- 60-90 minutes

What you need
- cards or small pieces of paper, markers
- large headings – "Helps", "Hinders", "Both", "Not Sure" – placed on the wall

How it's done
1. We explain the task: "In groups of two, discuss the key forces or elements ranged against you in your struggle at the moment and your major supports/allies. Choose four of the most important (two "for" and two "against") and note them on the cards in headline form. You have twenty minutes."
2. We give each pair four cards and some coloured markers.
3. After twenty minutes, we explain how to post the cards in the four columns on the wall: "Helps, Hinders, Both, Not Sure." We ask the first group to post their cards and to explain how each force or element is helping or hindering their struggles. If it is both helping and hindering, place it under "both". Subsequent groups should place their cards in relation to what is already there.
4. When all the cards are posted, we reflect on the "Hinders" column. We usually ask, "What's missing?" and "What are the common threads?" We might also ask the group to summarize the dominant agenda (what we're up against).
5. We look at the other columns to pinpoint key elements for a discussion of strategy:
   - in "Helps", who are our allies? What are some stories of resistance or of how we've already worked together?
   - how can we turn the "Both" and "Not Sure" forces into "Helps"?
   - how can we find the "cracks" in the dominant agenda to turn them into "Helps"?

Variations
- For other ways to analyse the balance of forces, See Barndt, *Naming the Moment.*
- "Helps/Hinders" can be adapted to many themes. For instance, when we used the activity in workshops with educators we change the question to "What helps/hinders our learning?"

Source
- DMI.

Nightmares

Why use it?
- to identify and analyse anticipated tensions in working as a social change educator
- to see how workshop design and/or facilitation can address those tensions

Time it takes
- 90 minutes (with about 20 people)

What you need
- workspaces for small groups of 4-5 people

How it's done
1. We explain the purpose of the exercise, hand out a tasksheet, and review the instructions.

Tasksheet: Nightmares of running a workshop/meeting
- Share your worst experiences or worst fears in running a workshop or other event.
- Develop a **five-minute** scenario or situation to illustrate the major points made in the discussion. Build on one person's story that resonated with others in the group, or develop a composite story.
- Prepare to dramatize this scenario to the other groups. You can use props, make signs, whatever you think will help your presentation.
2. We divide participants into groups of four or five persons and assign a workspace.
3. After thirty minutes we check to see whether everyone is ready. We allocate a few more minutes if necessary.
4. In turn the groups present their dramas. We usually give a warning at four minutes, and explain in advance that we will be cutting the action after five minutes. Otherwise it drags.
5. After each presentation there is discussion, using a couple of questions, and with notes made on the flip-chart:
- Name the nightmares you saw in the drama.
- Review what (if anything) the group tried to do to address the problems.
6. We give the participants five minutes back in their small groups to discuss how the presenting group might have dealt with the problems dramatized. They come back to the large group and share these ideas; again we note them on the flip-chart. After that we move on to the next drama.
7. After the last drama the facilitator leads a short summary reflection by the group, noting:
- common threads
- insights on the role of design and facilitation in solving the problems.

Variations
- Some of the presentations can be restaged, applying the suggestions made for solving the problems. (See also the activity "Stop drama".)

Source
- DMI.

The power flower: reflection on our social identities

Why use it?
■ to identify who we are (and who we aren't) as individuals and as a group in relation to those who wield power in our society.
■ to establish discrimination as a process for maintaining dominant identities.

Time it takes
■ 45-60 minutes

What you need
■ the power flower drawn on large paper
■ individual copies of the flower as handouts
■ a variety of coloured markers

How it's done
1. We introduce the power flower, which we have drawn on large paper and placed on the wall. Together we all fill in the dominant social identity of the group on the outside circle.
2. Asking people to work with the person next to them, we hand out individual flowers to each pair. We ask participants to locate themselves on the inner blank circle.
3. The groups of two post their identities on the inner circle of the large flower as soon as they are ready to do so.
4. We review the composite as a group and reflect on:

■ personal location: how many factors you have as an individual that are different from the dominant identity; what factors can't be shifted, changed?
■ representation: who we are/are not as a group – and how that might influence the task/discussion at hand.
■ the relationship between and among different forms of oppression.
■ the process at work to establish dominance of a particular identity and, at the same time, to subordinate other identities.

Variations
■ Individuals fill in the inner circle of the flower before reflecting on the dominant social identity in the group.
■ Using flip-chart paper, cut out large versions of the twelve different petals. Each petal should be large enough so that all participants can make an entry on it. Name each of the petals and spread them around the room. Participants circulate and record their personal identity on the inner part of the petal and the dominant identity on the outer part. Gather the petals in the centre of the room, and use as a catalyst for discussion as above.
■ Use the power flower as an introduction to focus on one form of oppression. The flower was developed specifically for use in anti-racist work.
■ List the words participants use to describe their own "ethnicity" and "race". Examine the two columns for differences. Use this as a take-off point for talking about race as a social – as opposed to scientific – concept.

Source
■ Barb Thomas, DMI. Adapted from *Lee, Letters to Marcia.*

The power flower

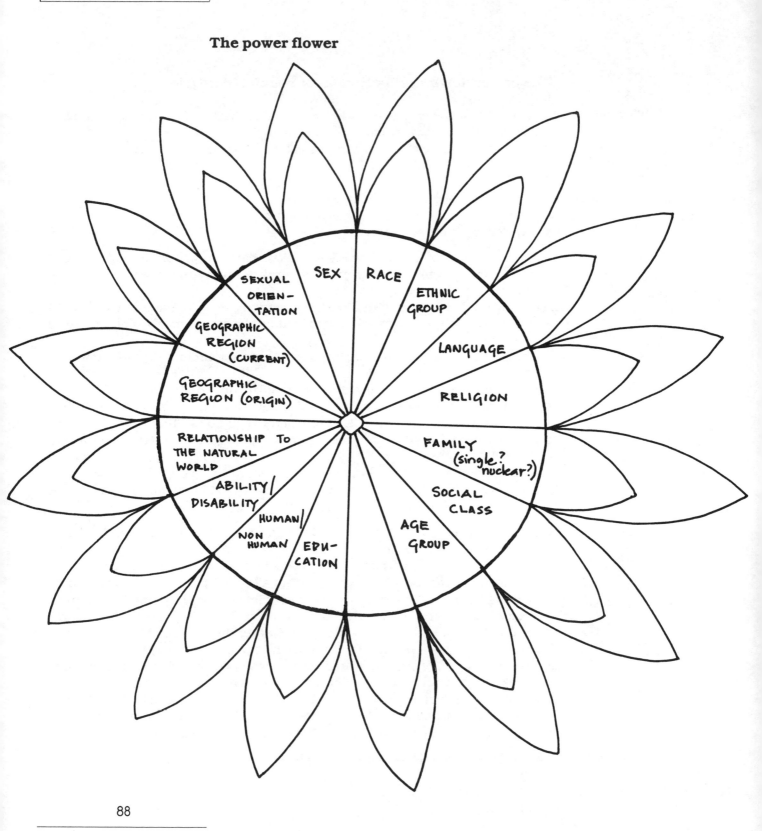

Drawing "When I see, hear, feel these things ..."

Why use it? ■ to identify connections between racism in the society and in the workplace

Time it takes ■ 60-90 minutes (with about 20 people)

What you need ■ work areas for four groups
■ large paper, coloured markers for each group

How it's done
1. We divide participants into four groups.
2. We give tasksheet A to groups #1 and #2 and tasksheet B to groups #3 and #4.
3. We explain the task, which is to either prepare a drawing of how racism happens in society or how it happens in the workplace. If people are intimidated by drawing, we suggest they draw with their non-dominant hand or that they sketch their own ideas on scrap paper and then work with others to develop a collective drawing.
4. We give large sheets of flip-chart paper and coloured markers to each group.
5. After thirty minutes we ask the groups to post their drawings. Beginning with the "society" drawings, we ask the other groups to identify what they see in the drawings and get the artists themselves to explain the main messages. All the points are noted on the flip-chart under "Society" and "Workplace" headings.
6. We ask participants to comment on any patterns they see in the drawings and data generated: for example, power, exclusion, or similarities between racism in society and in the workplace
7. We help participants frame this discussion using the triangle tool.

Variations
■ The activity can also be used to generate data on sexism and other forms of oppression.
■ The activity can be done as a collage instead of a drawing.
■ It may be important to talk about the process of doing the drawing before the discussion, especially if there has been discomfort in the room. A way to start might be to ask: "What was going on in your group as you tried to do the task together? Was it comfortable or uncomfortable?" This allows participants to put some words to difficult feelings.
■ Rather than doing a drawing, participants can be divided into six groups, each with a different point to consider:

❑ when I **see** in society ...   ❑ when I **see** in the workplace ...
❑ when I **hear** in society ...   ❑ when I **hear** in the workplace ...
❑ when I **feel** in society ...   ❑ when I **feel** in the workplace ...

■ Each of the six groups records its comments on flip-chart paper for the larger group to see. The facilitator proceeds with the discussion as above.

Source ■ Adapted by the DMI from Anne Marie Stewart, Toronto Board of Education.

Tasksheet A: racism in society

Prepare a group drawing to illustrate how racism happens **in our society,** outside our organizations. One way to help prepare the drawing is to discuss the following:

"When I see, hear, feel these things in the external environment, I know racism is happening."

You have thirty minutes to prepare.

Tasksheet B: racism in the workplace

Prepare a group drawing to illustrate how racism happens **inside our organizations.** One thing that may help you prepare the drawings is to discuss the following:

"When I see, hear, feel these things in my organization, I know racism is happening."

You have thirty minutes to prepare.

Triangle tool

Why use it?
■ to provide a framework for analysing connections and differences between systemic/structural, ideological, and personal aspects of racism

Time it takes
■ 30 minutes

What you need
■ flip-chart, markers, and tape
■ assumes prior discussion, such as the one described in the activity, Drawing "When I see, hear, feel these things..."

How it's done
1. We mark the three points of the triangle on the flip-chart: IDEAS, STRUCTURES/SYSTEMS, PERSONAL EXPERIENCE.
2. We draw a circle around each of the concepts, explaining each one as we go.
3. We ask participants to give us their comments from the "See, hear, feel" activity on racism in society, and we note these comments at the appropriate triangle point. There should be two or three comments for each point on the triangle.
4. We draw lines between the three triangle points and consider the relationship between them. We note that power operates at each point to maintain or challenge racism.
5. We ask participants to give their comments from the racism in their organizations drawings. We post these inside the triangle. We note down several comments until it is clear that the inside of our organizations reflects what is happening outside in society. We draw arrows to illustrate the connections.
6. In a brief synthesis we underline:
■ the need to address all three points on the triangle if we are to attack racism.
■ that what exists in society also exists in workplaces and other organizations.
■ Sometimes we also ask participants to consider the points in another group's drawing that they think should be added to their own analysis.

Variations
■ The activity can also be used to do an analysis of gender, race, ability – other forms of oppression.

Source
■ Barb Thomas, DMI.

The triangle tool

Here is an example of participants' comments that we've placed on the triangle.

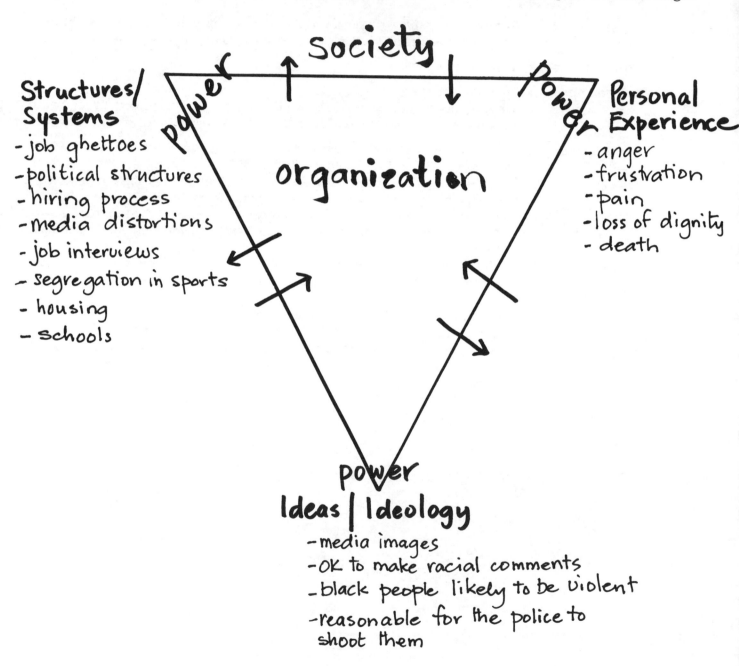

Facilitator presentations

Why use it?	■ to introduce the principles of education for social change and their basis in how people learn
Time it takes	■ 15-20 minutes
What you need	■ flip-charts prepared in advance on principles of effective adult education; principles of education for social change; and stages of a workshop (the spiral model)*
	■ flip-chart, markers, and tape
	■ prior exploration of participant experience in what makes education effective for them

How it's done

1. We make the charts ahead of time, including all of the main points we want to make. We also make visible the main points that emerged from the discussion of participant experience with effective education. (We often do this by having people share what helps and hinders them learn.)
2. We post the charts on principles of effective adult education and principles of education for social change. In reviewing the principles, we try to link them to the points already raised by the participants. The fact that many of these points have already been mentioned emphasizes that much of this information is knowledge they already had. What the presentation tries to do is suggest a framework.
3. We look at how this relates to the theory of how people learn by drawing the "learning heads" on the flip-chart. (See chapter two, "TAKING OURSELVES SERIOUSLY, Why we find the spiral model useful.")
4. We relate all of this to how we structure a learning event by presenting the spiral stages of a workshop – which both takes into account and uses the principles of education for social change and what we know about how people learn.
5. People are invited throughout to stop us and ask questions if there is something that is not clear.
6. We leave time following the presentation for questions, comments, and synthesis.

Variations ■ There are many other kinds of presentations: an outside resource person, use of a film or video, a panel ... the list is long. These presentations can be framed so that participants are active co-presenters in the process; the participants can seek what they want to learn rather than just what the presenter wants to say.

Source ■ DMI.

* All of these charts appear earlier in this chapter.

Sculpturing an analysis

This activity gets people to position themselves in ways expressing power relationships among major actors – in this example, among the major actors in the conflict in South Africa. The result is a human sculpture that represents the group's understanding and knowledge of what is going on in South Africa. In this case, South African resource people and facilitators with recent experience in the region added their information to that of participants.

Why use it?
■ to identify the major players in the conflict in South Africa and share information about their strategies
■ to critically examine Canada's role and our role as solidarity organizations in relation to the major South African actors

Time it takes
■ 45-60 minutes

What you need
■ at least 10 participants
■ two facilitators or a participant willing to assist one facilitator
■ a large space
■ small pieces of paper, masking tape, magic markers
■ flip-chart

How it's done
1. We ask participants to name the major actors in the conflict in South Africa. (They can name individuals, forces, or organizations). One facilitator writes the actors named on the flip-chart, checking to be sure that everyone knows who the actor is but without getting into any lengthy discussion.
2. At the same time, using the marker, the other facilitator writes the names of the actors on small slips of paper. We try to group the actors as we go – into opposition groups, apartheid supporters, international actors, and so on.
3. The first facilitator reviews the purpose of the exercise and explains that we will be choosing people to represent the actors and positioning them as a sculpture, placing them according to their relative power over resources and decision-making. The whole group decides where each actor goes. Participants can use different gestures or props.
4. The second facilitator asks two participants to take the roles of two of the actors representing the apartheid structures, sticking the slips of paper naming the actors on their bodies with masking tape. The group discusses how these actors should be positioned in terms of their power relationship.
5. We proceed to identify and place the other actors, leaving the international actors – and especially Canada and the solidarity network – until last. (It is important that we are in the picture.) We continue to check with the group to see that everyone's points are being included in the analysis being developed and that everyone understands the relationships.
   Some of the most useful discussions occur when people differ. In one workshop in 1987 with anti-apartheid youth, both Black Consciousness Movement (BCM) and African National Congress (ANC) supporters were

among the participants. After much discussion and debate, we were able to agree on the historical and current positioning of each actor, naming differences in analysis as we went along.

6. We ask clarifying questions and add information where necessary.

7. Before we break up the sculpture and everyone sits down, we ask the actors to review who they are and how they relate to each other. (We find it's also helpful to ask how it feels to be in the role.)

8. We have a discussion, which often focuses on the role of the Canadian government and the implications for solidarity work.

Variations
■ Another sculpture could be made to represent how we would like to change the situation – how we would like the relationships to be – or to represent possible responses to the situation we've described.

■ This approach to sculpturing can be used to develop an analysis of one sector only (for instance, the trade union sector in South Africa, the food sector in Canada).

■ The "theatre of the oppressed" can also be used to look at contradictions in relations of power. For an example, see Barndt, *Naming the Moment*, pp.43-44.

Source
■ Rick Arnold and Bev Burke, DMI.

95

PRACTISING
SKILLS,
FORMING
STRATEGIES,
AND PLANNING
FOR ACTION

Using video

Why use it?
■ to document the practice of facilitation in training sessions with social change educators
■ to affirm and critique participants' own skills in facilitation
■ to enlist feedback from colleagues

Time it takes
■ 1 day for recording & feedback (assumes prior preparation)

What you need
■ video recorder and playback (1 set for every 8 participants)
■ videotape for each participant
■ one quiet work area for every 8 participants
■ flip-chart, pens, tape in each area
■ 1 facilitator for every 8 participants

How it's done
1. On the day before the session, in teams of two the participants prepare a design for a three-hour workshop for a particular constituency on a particular theme. On the day of the session the facilitators divide the collected pairs into two groups, with each facilitator responsible for four teams.
2. The facilitator explains the task. Each team is to present the outline of their workshop plan; and facilitate a ten-minute segment as if the facilitators were the participants.
3. The process for the videotaping is posted on a flip-chart:
■ team sets up
■ team explains the plan (general objectives, participants, agenda) and describes how the activity to be facilitated fits into the plan
■ the "audience" takes on the role of the participants
■ facilitation of the plan (ten minutes)
■ note-taking (five minutes)

Note: all the teams should present their segment and be taped, one after the other, in the morning before the feedback begins.
4. In the afternoon the full group generates guidelines for feedback. (This process is described in detail in chapter four, "GIVING AND GETTING FEEDBACK".) The facilitator asks, "What helps you hear critical feedback?" and notes participant input on the flip-chart. These notes become "guidelines for feedback", which are used to give critical feedback to colleagues on their presentations. The facilitator is responsible for making sure that the guidelines are followed.

5. We replay the videotapes and tape the feedback. For feedback we use this process:
- The team comments on what they thought they did well; what could have been improved; what they want comments/suggestions on.
- Each person in turn gives feedback according to the guidelines established. The team cannot answer back.
- After hearing all of the feedback, the presenters make summary comments (if time permits).
6. Each participant gets a tape of her or his presentation and feedback.

Variation ■ When no video equipment is available, we adapt the process: there is feedback immediately following each team presentation, using the same process as outlined above.

Source ■ DMI skillshops.

Case studies

For this example, we have chosen film clips used as case studies in a skillshop with educators from immigrant service organizations.

Why use it?
■ to practise using the triangle tool (see "ADDING THEORY OR NEW INFORMATION" in this chapter) for an analysis of equity issues (racism and sexism) in the workplace
■ to explore ways to use the case studies in dealing with issues and tensions common in educationals about equity

Time it takes
■ 90 minutes

What you need
■ 5-minute video clips – as case studies on workplace discrimination
■ group scenarios written on flip-chart
■ workspace for small groups

How it's done
1. We show two of the video clips: a case of sexual harassment of a woman worker in a hospital and a case of racism directed against a worker in a loading yard.
2. We post a number of different scenarios developed for using the case studies in educationals. These relate to the specific work contexts of the participants and to the case studies. Here are two scenarios that we've used:
■ for video #1 – sexual harassment "You have been asked to come and talk to female workers in the hospital about sexual harassment."
■ for video #2 – loading yard "You have been asked to prepare a session for the union at the loading yard to sensitize the workers to cross-cultural issues."
3. We hand out a tasksheet and review it with participants:
4. We ask participants to choose the scenario they wish to work on by voting with their feet – moving to the place in the room where that scenario is posted.
5. When all participants have made their choice we divide into groups so a maximum of four to five people are working together. A scenario has to be chosen by at least three people or it does not get used.
6. Groups get sixty minutes to complete the task, during which time the facilitator circulates.
7. We ask each group to post the triangle tool (if used) and answers to the questions posed; and to have one person prepared to answer questions from other participants.
8. Participants circulate in a gallery review of the work produced. We encourage groups that have worked on the same scenario to compare responses and new ideas or insights.
9. In plenary, we record a summary of "insights" and "blocks or problems" in doing the exercise.

Variations ■ Case studies can come in many formats: print, audio-visual, photostories. They can be used for many purposes as well. For example, we used a written case study of the Guatemala Coca Cola workers in workshops with Canadian food industry workers as a way of learning about other ways of building alliances.

Source ■ DMI. The video clips in this activity were from Workplace Discrimination, City of Toronto, 1987.

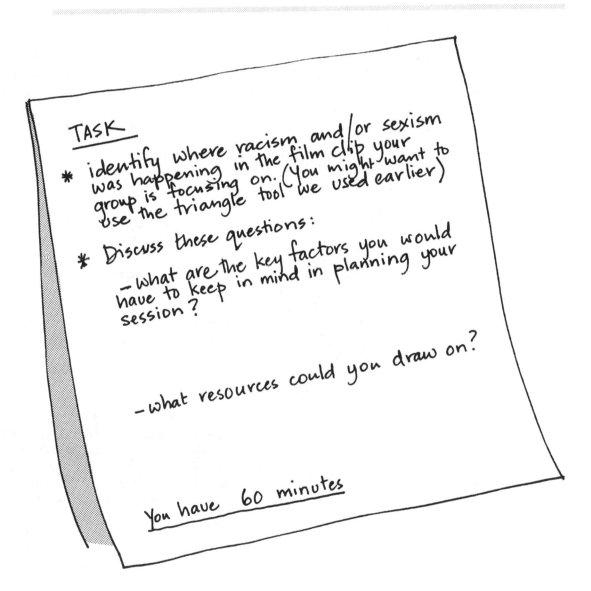

TASK

* identify where racism and/or sexism was happening in the film clip your group is focusing on. (You might want to use the triangle tool we used earlier)

* Discuss these questions:

– what are the key factors you would have to keep in mind in planning your session?

– what resources could you draw on?

You have 60 minutes

Stop drama, or "take two"

Why use it? ▪ to develop concrete strategies for dealing with conflict situations in our work as social change educators

Time it takes ▪ 90 minutes (with about 20 people)

What you need ▪ a large area, free of furniture
▪ space for 4 groups to work
▪ flip-chart, markers, tape

How it's done 1. We follow the procedure outlined in the "Nightmares" activity: participants divide into small groups and develop dramatizations of their worst experiences, of their fears about running a workshop, or of working with a group immersed in conflict.

2. Each group presents its scenario and the group as a whole identifies the nature of the conflict(s) they see dramatized. In one drama, for instance, there might be competing political perspectives, a facilitator trying to avoid conflict, and a generation-gap issue.

3. After all of the groups present their drama, we introduce the process that we're going to use for looking at strategies to address the issues raised. We explain that the time available allows us to only work with one or two of the dramas. So we ask participants to choose which one(s) they want to work on.

4. The original group presents the drama over again. Participants reconvene in their groups for ten minutes to develop concrete strategies for addressing the situation. We ask each group to name a facilitator who will try out the group strategy for dealing with the situation.

5. Each group has an opportunity to take the place of the facilitator in the scene and replay it in a different way, using the original group as the participants.

6. After all of the groups have had an opportunity to practise their strategies, the facilitator leads a discussion of the approaches that have emerged, noting the main points on the flip-chart.

Variations ▪ Any member of the audience who wants to intervene and become a character in the drama can do so by clapping her or his hands to stop the action. The new actor takes the place of someone in the drama and the action resumes.

▪ If someone feels that any response or action in the drama is unrealistic, she or he calls out "magic". This stops the drama, and the person intervening must enter the scene and replay it in a more realistic manner.

Source ▪ Adapted by members of the DMI from Theatre of the Oppressed approaches.

REFLECTION
AND
EVALUATION

Quick and dirty: reconstructing an activity

Why use it?
■ to reflect critically on an activity during an event, when the activity has not gone well.

Time it takes
■ 15-30 minutes

What you need
■ cards or small pieces of paper and markers

How it's done
1. In advance we break down the activity into its component parts, and we make a card for each point. We copy the cards so there are two identical sets.
2. We divide participants into two teams and give each team one set of cards. We ask them to put the activity cards into the right order – that is, the order in which the activity occurred.
3. When both groups have finished this task, they compare the reconstructions and work to reach an agreement on the order of the parts of the activity.
4. In smaller groups, participants are asked to identify what worked or didn't work in the original activity and why. We ask them if they have any suggestions for improvement.
5. Participants return to the plenary and report back on their discussions and suggestions.

Source
■ DMI.

EDUCATING FOR A CHANGE

Quick and dirty: line-up

This example is taken from a specific workshop looking at coalition-building on a national level in Canada. There was a wide range of participants from across the country.

Why use it? ■ to clarify objectives when there is disagreement among participants

Time it takes ■ 15 minutes + follow-up

How it's done 1. We asked two participants to represent the extreme poles. A participant who saw the purpose of the session as a time for people to listen to each other went to one side of the room. A participant who saw the objective as organizing an action campaign went to the other side.
2. When these two participants were in place, we asked others in the group to physically position themselves along the line between the two according to how they saw the objectives for the session.
3. We asked people to briefly explain the reasons for their position.
4. Based on this information, we asked the participants to look at the agenda and see how their differing priorities could be covered. We agreed on making changes to the agenda.

Variations ■ Have people line up by the length of time they have been with the organization. It gives a sense of both new blood and experience in the room.
■ The activity can be used as a conflict resolution technique to come up with a compromise solution.
■ It can also be used for the quick and dirty end-of-session evaluations: one end of the line for "absolutely wonderful"; the other end for "yuck".

Source ■ Adapted and readapted by many different groups. Special thanks to Denise Nadeau, a popular educator in Vancouver.

Fly on the ceiling

We gave the exercise this name to indicate the need for participants to step out of the process and look at it from a distance.

Why use it?
■ to determine to what extent the process and content of an event are meeting the needs of participants

Time it takes
■ 10-30 minutes at the end of a day/session

What you need
■ a copy of the "fly on the ceiling" handout for each person for each day of the event

How it's done
1. We give each participant a copy of the handout and explain the purpose of the exercise. We note that the sheet is for their own reference and will not be collected.
2. As a group, we reconstruct the day by reviewing what happened.
3. We give participants five minutes to fill in the sheet.
4. We either ask for volunteers or ask all participants to comment on what happened for them during the day; what worked or didn't work. We stress that this information will help us redesign the program for the next day.

Variations
■ Focus on a particular problem that emerged during the day.
■ Participants can be asked to say what they want the program to stop, start, keep doing the next day.

Source
■ DMI.

Fly on the ceiling

1. What did we do (reconstruction)? Why?

2. What happened for you – summarize what you learned or felt.

3. What could you use? How could you change it to meet your own situation? What alternatives can you think of?

Process observers

Why use it?	■ to give participants an opportunity to practice observing and critiquing process
	■ to equalize power relations between facilitator and participants
Time it takes	■ 10 minutes for the report
What you need	■ Copies of the "process observer sheet"
How it's done	1. In the first session of a longer event, during the introduction to the program, we introduce the "process observer" concept and its objective and review the sheet with the group.
	2. We ask for two volunteers for the first day of the program. We explain that these two process observers are responsible for collecting input from other participants, and that they will make a short report at the beginning of the session following the one they observed.
	3. The process observer report is the first thing we usually ask for in the morning, before reviewing the agenda for the day. Then we ask for new volunteers to act as process observers for the coming session.
Variations	■ Depending on the sector, we may change the title. In the union movement the role of class steward can be adapted to take on this role.
Source	■ DMI.

Process observer sheet

Your role:

1. To be available to participants for input into the course as we go along.
2. To reflect on how the day went, keeping in mind:
■ participation
■ pacing (Did things move too fast? too slow?)
■ balance of new and familiar content
■ language (Could everyone understand? Is the terminology clear?)
■ logistics.

At the end of the day, prepare your report with the other observer based on feedback from other participants and your own observations during the day. The report should be no more than ten minutes in length and will be given at the beginning of the morning session. You might want to make your observations on this sheet.

Head, heart, feet

Why use it? ■ to evaluate a session at its conclusion

Time it takes ■ 30 minutes

What you need ■ evaluation sheet for each participant
■ flip-chart, markers, tape

How it's done 1. We hand out the evaluation sheet, explaining its objective and how the information will be used.
2. We invite participants to draw their head, heart, feet on the paper, using the markers.
3. We ask participants to fill in the form (individually or with someone else).
4. If there is time, we ask them to share something they learned or to give final comments.

Variations ■ Draw a large head, heart, feet on flip-chart paper and post it. Distribute small slips of paper and ask participants to write down the major things they learned or got out of the event. Post these points in the appropriate position on the flip-chart and discuss them.

Source ■ Adapted from Marsha Sfeir, a Toronto educator. The variation was developed by participants at a workshop in Peterborough, Ontario.

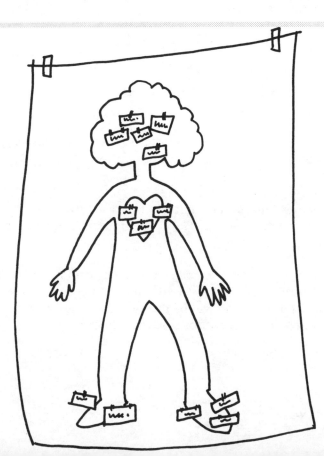

Educating for a change: course evaluation

Date:

This form has two purposes. We hope it will help you reflect on your own learning during the course. We know it will help us improve our work. To make the evaluation as useful as possible to us, it helps if you can be specific and personal (for instance, use "I" instead of "we").

Part one: What did you learn from this course?

a) New knowledge gained from the course; new questions you would like answers to
b) New understandings, feelings, you leave with
c) New skills – things you can use in your work

Part two: Your assessment of the course

1. What parts of the course did you find most useful? Why?
2. What parts did you find least useful? Why?
3. What ideas could you suggest for improvement?

Many thanks for taking the time to fill this out.

ENERGIZING
PARTICIPANTS
AND
FACILITATORS

The people say

Why use it? ■ to deal with sluggishness during a workshop/meeting/event

Time it takes ■ 2-5 minutes

What you need ■ no additional requirements

How it's done
1. We explain to people that we have noticed glazed eyes or feel tired ourselves – whatever has prompted us to introduce the exercise. We also explain that there is a physiological reason for the exercise: to get oxygen to the brain.
2. We explain the game. "I will be asking you to take an action. Because we are concerned about democratic social change here, we want the people involved in our decisions. So, respond to my request only if I preface it with 'the people say'. For example, if I say 'the people say, stand up', you stand up. If I only say 'stand up', you pay no attention."
3. We do the exercise. We don't have people drop out if they miss the trick because the idea is to get some exercise.

Source ■ "Simon says" – with a twist, thanks to theatre workers from the Eastern Caribbean.

Post Office

Why use it? ■ to deal with sluggishness during a session – and to have fun

Time it takes ■ 5-10 minutes

What you need ■ chairs in a circle, one for each participant with the facilitator's chair removed
■ a piece of paper

How it's done 1. We explain the purpose of the exercise, its name, and where it comes from.
2. We outline the rules. We explain that the facilitator is a letter carrier with a letter (the piece of paper). We say, "I have a letter here for everyone with hair on their heads – and the amount of hair doesn't matter." Everyone answering this description changes chairs across the circle (and not just shifts sideways). We explain that the facilitator will also be looking for a chair. The person without the chair becomes the new letter carrier.
3. We continue until everyone looks more or less awake.

■ **A caution:** This activity is not appropriate for groups with participants who are unable to move quickly and easily from chair to chair.

Source ■ Popular educators in Central America in the Alforja network.

Sentence reconstruction

Why use it? ▪ as a warm-up before a session

Time it takes ▪ 15 minutes

What you need ▪ each word from 2 sentences written on different index cards

How it's done
1. We choose sentences that relate to the theme of the session.
2. We divide the participants into two teams, and give each team a set of cards.
3. We explain that the task is to reconstruct the sentence.
4. When both teams have finished, we ask them to show the sentence to the other team.

Variations
▪ Both teams could work with the same sentence.
▪ Use the exercise to spark a discussion of working collectively by reflecting on what helped get the task done or what blocked its progress.

Source ▪ DMI.

Person to person

Why use it? ▪ to deal with sluggishness during a session or as an icebreaker

Time it takes ▪ 10 minutes

What you need ▪ an odd number of people

How it's done
1. We ask participants to choose a partner and stand in a large circle.
2. Borrowing a partner, a facilitator explains the rules and demonstrates how it's done. When we call out two parts of the body (for instance, hand to head) one person puts her hand on the head of her partner. We continue to call out different combinations until people are tangled up. At that point we shout "person to person" and everyone changes partners. The person without a partner becomes the new caller.
3. We begin the exercise, calling, for instance, "knee to hip, toe to toe, shoulder to ankle" – until everyone is tangled. Then we call "person to person" and find a partner ourselves. A participant becomes the new caller.
4. We continue as long as we have time available, or until it threatens to become boring.

Source ▪ Sticks and Stones theatre group, Sudbury, Ontario. ("Personne à personne" is described in their book *Neighbourhood Action: Recipes for Change* (out of print).

111

A FINAL WORD

We hope you will use and adapt these activities for your own work. And as you do, don't forget the checklist for developing appropriate activities.

Consider

- the local context
- the number of participants
- who the participants are: their cultural background, sector, social class, race, gender, traditions
- "comfort level" – would participants feel uncomfortable doing the activity at this stage in the event?
- objectives
- the design – when in the workshop should the activity take place? to get out participant experience, analyse a topic, add new information, make an action plan?
- the time of day
- the time you have
- language-level and literacy
- space, logistics
- materials and technology available or required
- theme or subject matter
- resources you have
- participant experience, how much they know about the theme
- organizational context (timing, who is involved)
- your nightmares, and potential resistance to the activity

4

Working On Our Feet:
The Practice of Democratic Facilitation

6 LOOKING FORWARD: Implications for our work in the 1990's

5 LOOKING BACK: Issues emerging from our practice

3 SHAPING OUR TOOLS: Developing and Using Activities

2 WORKING BY DESIGN: Putting together a program

4 WORKING ON OUR FEET: The practice of democratic facilitation

1 THIS IS OUR CHANCE: Educating Strategically

So here you are. You're well prepared. But you're facing fifteen or twenty-five people who have differing expectations of the workshop and who want to be there in varying degrees. They see you as the expert but may resent and want to challenge the very status they've accorded you.

They will participate in and resist the process in different ways. They will blame you if "it doesn't work". A few of them – probably the ones who have invited you to run the workshop – may be hoping that you will ring up the political points they've been unable to score with these, their colleagues.

Indeed, as we mentioned in chapter one, there can be many agendas – your own included – operating in one simple workshop. Clarity on where these connect and diverge will help you negotiate traffic, on your feet, and avoid getting bogged down.

After all, the contradictions are the very essence of what you're doing: facilitation. And book after book, it seems, has been written about how to pick your way through this potential swamp. In this chapter we're going to address eight aspects of facilitation in social change education:

✧ the use of space
✧ making the most of who we are
✧ establishing credibility and challenging notions of the expert
✧ getting and giving feedback
✧ encouraging/challenging resistance
✧ working with discomfort
✧ dealing with conflict
✧ timing.

RICK ARNOLD

We're focusing on these eight issues for three reasons.

First, social change education challenges ourselves and the people in our programs to refocus and reframe "common-sense" understandings and questions about what is happening in our society. It challenges us to consider why these things happen, how they happen, what their impact is and on whom, and what our own location is in these dynamics. In educational work the eight aspects are sites where, in our experience, responses to these issues are played out.

Second, social change education is about developing democratic practice. The eight sites pose some of the most challenging problems for the educator in modelling democratic practice.

Third, mainstream adult education literature abounds with ideas for managing troublesome individuals. But little has been written about facilitator roles in developing critically aware individuals equipped to recognize and resist injustices.

And fourth, we want to affirm conflict in groups as something natural, potentially creative, and necessary in building collectivities capable of working together effectively.

When you start a session there are always some dynamics you can anticipate, and you've taken these into account in your planning and design. But there is a universe of undocumented, on-your-feet experiences that are not only contradictory but also filled with tension, and sometimes painful. We want to explore these swampy places in this chapter.

As authors we are aware of a central tension in this chapter. On the one hand we wanted to make the job of facilitation accessible to anyone attempting it, by analysing its most difficult aspects. On the other hand, the more we probed such moments and tried to illustrate approaches to them, the more we realized that these descriptions might, in fact, overwhelm and disempower some readers.

To this we respond that there is a craft to facilitation, most of which is learned on your feet. While it is true that "anyone can do this", we have found that one gets better and better through experience and through shared reflection with trusted colleagues. It is this shared reflection, at this point in our work, that we offer here.

USING SPACE:
THE POLITICS
OF FURNITURE

A story

A union invites two educators to provide training in popular education for some of their staff. When the educators arrive for the session they see a room formally set up with a big table at the front, complete with a microphone, and with all of the chairs organized auditorium-fashion, facing the microphone. (The chairs, they notice, are movable).

Hiding their dismay, they ask if this is the normal arrangement for a workshop room and are told that yes it is and that the union president will be opening the session. They raise no challenge.

The president's opening remarks signal his support for the event and thus provide the psychological space for the educators to move.

After his opening speech the participants wait expectantly for the educators' presentation. After all, the room is organized for someone to present something. The educators, maintaining the given arrangement, negotiate objectives and an agenda. Then they organize the participants into pairs to discuss expectations, after which individuals share their responses and ideas with the group as a whole. While this is happening people crane and twist their necks to see who is speaking.

Next the participants go off to the four corners of the room for small-group work in which they are to develop a role-play. Later, when they reassemble for presentation of the role-plays, participants rearrange the chairs so they can see.

By noon the room looks very different. In response to the need to see everyone's faces in a large-group session, participants had arranged their chairs in a circle, with facilitators as members of the group. At some point in the morning almost every corner of the room had been used.

Before lunch the facilitators ask participants to comment on the room arrangement and to compare it to the beginning of the morning. Participants comment that they like the current arrangement much better. They could talk and hear easier and see everyone's faces, including the facilitators'.

They begin, right away, to reflect on their own use of space and furniture in union meetings. Participants agree that they would have resisted such an arrangement if it had been imposed by the facilitators at the beginning of the morning. They say it would have confirmed their suspicions about the "touchy-feely" outsiders.

So what's going on?

The use of space is a statement about power relations in an organization. In larger organizations, power is displayed by office, window, carpet, space, and equipment allocations.

In a structured educational setting, the arrangement of furniture – conscious or not – makes power relations apparent. It shows these power relations in the anticipation of who will be talking, and who will be listening. While people may, at one level, resent being talked to all the time, they may also take some security in the predictability of such an arrangement, and in the position it affords as an observer. An arbitrary shift made by an outsider to the organization can be experienced as an affront to tradition, to "the way we do things".

Such feelings, especially when they're fuelled at the outset of an educational experience that is already unpredictable and slightly uncomfortable, can derail the most engaging and exciting design.

Facilitators, then, need to walk a bit of a tightrope. On the one hand they must model the respect for people and their ways of doing things that is the basis of education for social change. On the other hand they must help participants raise questions about how such "innocent" arrangements reflect the very inequities that social change education seeks to challenge.

But if participants themselves are to create democratic spatial arrangements in their own work, they must consciously participate in the creation of these arrangements, in response to felt needs. Any layout favours some people at the expense of others. The trick is to develop skills in assessing and shifting who is favoured. For example, if you have two flip-charts at the front of a room you can angle your body in two different ways for each flip-chart, so you'll favour different people at different points.

ALOK MUKHERJEE

Tips on using space democratically

✦ **Do your homework.** In your planning, ask about the usual spatial arrangements for educational sessions in the place you're going to, and how open to change participants might be.

✦ **Request the kind of space you need.** If possible, see the space in advance or request a full description. Ask about the size, and if there are windows, carpets, and wall space for flip-chart paper.

Ask about disruptive noise. Request an additional room for small-group work; and a lounge for evenings if you're teaching a residential course. Get there early enough to ensure that you get the space you need, and that it is set up appropriately.

✦ **Use your design to shift things.** Use different activities to get participants to move their bodies and chairs and to use as many parts of the room as possible. Share the power to get up and move around.

✦ **Occasionally move the "front" of the room.** Following a group-work activity, get participants to report, using their own flip-chart notes, from wherever they are sitting. If you need to be standing or commenting, move to where the participants are.

✦ **Where possible, use the floor.** Many activities are designed for the floor. (See, for example, one of the variations in "The power flower" in chapter three.) Where there are no tables, and/or where the floor is carpeted, participants will often choose to work with flip-chart paper on the floor, which can also expand the use of space in the room.

✦ **Encourage participants to use the walls.** Activities that require participants to post comments, write graffiti, or assemble bits of data are occasions for encouraging participants to claim new spaces in the room. After an activity you may want to post particular sections of the flip-chart work for future reference in the workshop. Make sure you do this selectively so you won't drown participants in their own work.

✦ **Share the "props".** Share the tools you are using. Avoid maintaining a bank of markers, masking tape, folders, and flip-chart paper that only you as facilitator can touch or use.

✦ **Make the process explicit.** Spatial arrangements are not accidental, whether conscious or not. Particularly if you are training other educators, make time to pose specific questions about the "politics of furniture".

◇ Who is set up to talk and/or to listen in the spatial arrangement?
◇ In what ways can certain arrangements reinforce or undermine relations of power?
◇ What kinds of arrangements assist democratic processes?
◇ How do numbers of people, tasks to be accomplished, levels of comfort influence the spatial arrangements we choose?
◇ How can education for social change build comfort in spatial arrangements that encourage a sharing of power?

MAKING THE
MOST OF WHO
WE ARE

A story

Three facilitators who work together extensively – one Black, one South Asian, one White – are working with a group of teachers in the second stage of training in anti-racist work. Just before beginning in the afternoon, the teachers discuss who will make presentations to the Board of Education about hiring people of colour in senior positions at the Board.

A Black teacher is trying to sign up different people for the task. The group suggests several people, none of whom are at the meeting. One of the facilitators asks, "Why are you only naming people who are not here? What about the people who are here?"

The group looks uncomfortable, and then a few White teachers suggest that the first Black teacher along with another Black teacher should do the job. The first Black teacher confronts the group, saying, "It's always people of colour who have to do this. If you think it's less risky for us, you're very mistaken. This is exactly why it's hard to trust White people's good intentions sometimes."

One White group member protests "being made to feel guilty". "It's clear," he said, "that you (indicating the two Black women) are more experienced in this than I am."

One of the Black women responds, "What I'm getting here is that even in this group, racism is still our issue. Don't you think we're afraid we'll say the wrong thing, or that this will have repercussions for our jobs? In fact, we're more likely to get nailed than you are."

The three facilitators look at each other. They can see that the greatest discomfort is surfacing among the White participants. It is clear that some work is required with the White participants, while they remain in the large group.

The Black facilitator, who had heard this conversation all too often, signals, simultaneously, her support and her intent to observe. The South Asian facilitator works inside the organization and both his racial and organizational identities make a lead role in this situation problematic for him.

A judgement has to be made, based on trust. A formal time-out is not possible, so in a few glances the situation is settled. The White facilitator moves her chair to a different spot, indicating her willingness to structure the ensuing discussion.

The group spends two hours looking at what is going on. Individual Whites in the group examine what they would want to say if they were to make a presentation to the Board. They look at what made them afraid to do this, and under what conditions they might overcome such a fear. They examine the impact of their behaviour on their colleagues of colour and talk about the requirements for building real trust between Whites and people of colour in fighting racism.

Through all of this the people of colour in the room maintain a watchful distance, occasionally posing questions of clarification and supportive challenge to the White people.

Following the program, many participants, including the facilitators, send letters and attend the meetings where hiring is discussed.

119

So what's going on?   In this story there are three identities: social (in this case racial); organizational insider/outsider; and educational (in this case, transformational educator).

Social identity

Whether the social issue is class, gender, North-South relations, disability, or race, your own location in the oppressed or oppressor group matters. (See the discussion of the power flower in chapter one.)

In this case the White facilitator could have confirmed the distrust of White participants that was building in the room by avoiding the issue or moving on to another item. At such times, even the closest of friends and allies can suddenly feel themselves as "part of the problem" or "part of the oppressed group" – on opposite sides of the room.

At the same time, it would have been entirely inappropriate for the White facilitator to have spoken for or on behalf of the people of colour in the room. It would have been equally inappropriate for her to have focused the discussion on the behaviour of the Black women in the room, when they had taken all the risks in the discussion so far.

But the White facilitator could play a useful role in encouraging Whites to name what was going on and to probe the reasons and impact of their behaviour. As a White person she knew this experience firsthand. As a White person her racial identity did not distract the White participants from their own task of examining the impact of racism on themselves. She could use her racial identity to move the process forward.

There are just as many occasions when it is the facilitator who is a woman, a person of colour, or a Native person who is best placed to address the particular issue, tension, or question arising. Trying to read the signals correctly, to find out when it is best to play what role, is an important part of our work as educators. And this work is essential in building relations with the colleagues we are working with.

Organizational insider/outsider

Being inside or outside the organization also matters. Within organizations there are particular risks and benefits in challenging the way things are. Inside facilitators, as employees or members of organizations, share those costs. They can talk from or allude to their experience.

Outside facilitators are not subject to the same constraints and must therefore avoid glib analyses of the consequences of action. They will not bear the penalties. Their clarity about this is essential if participants who do work inside the organization are to trust their leadership in analysing and developing appropriate action.

Both insiders and outsiders need each other. But they must be respectful of the constraints on – as well as the possibilities for – the other's actions.

Educational identity – transformational

Social change educators have a stake in the outcome of conflicts. They are not "neutral" facilitators. For social change educators, participants are often also colleagues and allies. There are times to take an appropriate distance. If the educator is an organizational outsider, the risks are greater for the organizational members planning the action than for the facilitator. As participants weigh both their fears and the consequences of particular actions or inaction, the social change educator's role is to help them clarify what those risks are likely to be and to help them make decisions based on their own sense of the consequences. The role is not to preach about what people should do.

BARB THOMAS

BARB THOMAS

Tips on making the most of who we are

✦ **Clarify and name whether you are a target of the oppression or a member of the dominant group.** This has implications for your sources of knowing about this form of oppression, and for the sources of your credibility in challenging it.

This does not mean that as a member of the dominant group (for example, men) you cannot choose to fight that form of oppression. At different moments, and in different groups, you may gain credibility for being connected with either the dominant or oppressed group.

✦ **Clarify your interests.** In the case of racism, people of colour and White people are hurt by racism differently.

People of colour are its targets. All too often they are additionally burdened with the responsibility of educating Whites about it. They may resent doing so, and they may be resented for doing so.

Whites are diminished by their inability to locate the ways in which racism hurts them, and by the distrust provoked by their reluctance to take the consequences for challenging racism.

As an organizational insider/outsider, and as a transformational educator, you also have particular interests. These need to be clear to you as well as to participants.

✦ **Name your fears.** If you, as a facilitator, are a member of the target group, you may already fear the sustained and continuing expressions of the oppression you face.

In addition, the labelling, marginalizing, and dismissing of your efforts to bring about change may further frustrate you and have an impact on your work. However, clarity about these considerations in your work can inform and assist others seeking to work with you.

For example, as a woman inside a male-dominated union, you may want to engage an outside male educator to work with male staff on the issue of sexual harassment. This educator needs to know how to avoid making conditions worse for you while at the same time challenging the men to look critically at harassment.

✦ **Seek appropriate roles for yourself.** Depending on your identity as dominant group or non-dominant group member, or as organizational insider or outsider, it may be appropriate to either support the discussion from the sidelines or play a front-line role.

Even when two educators with different identities work together, they can adopt tactics for who does the processing and who injects new content. Avoid, for example, always having the non-dominant group member provide the content and theory about that form of oppression while the dominant group member provides the processing.

✦ **Model equity in your working relationships.** This means constantly monitoring your participation in a program to see if it is reinforcing or challenging inequities.

In your working relationships you can make sure your education team is composed of dominant and non-dominant identities, regardless of the subject under discussion. (Often people with non-dominant identities are sought only for their expertise on the form of oppression they experience.)

Watch that the roles you play in your educational work do not reinforce stereotypes. As an educator on your feet, you will also have to deal with how a group treats both you and one or more other facilitators, and how you can challenge dominant perceptions and practice.

In addition, check which authors are reflected in your readings; who appears, who speaks in your audio-visuals; who has the opportunity to attend workshops; how publicity and registration processes can promote equity.

✦ **Don't freeze yourself into a role.** There are no axioms for selecting when it is appropriate to play a particular role, based on one's particular identities. For example, it may be useful for a White person to do anti-racist work for a while, with other Whites in a White-dominated organization. There may come a time when a more appropriate role is to coach or make way for people of colour who are already skilled in the work, and then move on.

✦ **Make sure your own learning has varied sources.** There are decided limits to what you can know about poverty if you are a middle-class person, or about gender inequities if you are male. Identify the limits and strengths of your position.

Work with colleagues who can challenge you to extend your range, expand what you see, and use your strengths.

✦ **Watch for co-optation by participants.** Some participants who share your social identity may express certain expectations about you "being on their side", or of you "understanding where they are coming from". Use this as an entry point for helpful challenge rather than for unthinking alignment.

RICK ARNOLD

ESTABLISHING
CREDIBILITY /
SHARING THE
EXPERT ROLE

A story

A parent-teacher association organizes an evening workshop on the role of the media in shaping children's perceptions of gender roles. They hope to emerge with some actions they can take. A steering committee is charged with finding a resource person to run the evening. One of the members suggests an educator he knows who has done some work on this and who would run a participatory session.

The educator meets with the steering committee to clarify their objectives and to find out about the participants and their needs. She then writes up a brief description of the objectives and the process for the workshop and sends the outline back to the committee for further discussion. They approve her outline by telephone and she suggests a way of publicizing the workshop and doing the introductions.

On the evening of the workshop a steering committee member who had not attended the planning meeting introduces her. He refers to her, briefly, as an educator who has done a great deal of work on equity issues and then turns the workshop over to the "guest resource person".

A parent raises his hand and says he hadn't come to talk about racism, he'd come to "hear about how the media worked".

The educator, a Southeast Asian, suggests that someone else from the steering committee say something about her meeting with them and the planning process. Following a few additional comments by steering committee members, the educator asks if she can continue. After getting support to do so, she quickly negotiates objectives and clarifies the process she intends to use. People agree.

By way of introducing the subject the educator asks participants to group themselves, first by the media they spend most time with and second by the media their children spend most time with. A lively discussion follows, touching on the discrepancies between parents and children in both the form and content of media they watch and read.

After a while the same man interrupts again and says he had come to hear someone who knew something about the media speak about it. He had not come to play games. The educator calmly indicates that she is addressing the objectives agreed to by the steering committee and approved by the group. She asks if other participants feel the same way as the man. One woman states firmly that she doesn't. She says she had half expected a presentation but was finding the discussion stimulating, and she wanted more. Others agree.

The educator points to copies of two articles on the media she had brought and gives the man a copy of each of them. "Nobody wants to waste their time," she says to him. "If you feel you'll be wasting yours, I won't be offended if you want to call it a night and take the articles with you. However, in my experience you can get factual information from a variety of sources. It is analysing what that information means for what we do that is difficult. We can use our time together to help each other with that."

124

So what's going on?

There is a tension between the need to establish credibility and the need to challenge the notion of the expert. Yet to work effectively and democratically the educator for social change must do both.

Let's consider four of the major issues arising from this situation: social identity and the image of the expert; the role of the insider in establishing the credibility of the outsider; reconciling the agenda with participant expectations; and the notion that learning is listening to someone who knows.

The image of the expert

In this case the educator had anticipated difficulty in establishing credibility. These difficulties might have arisen from four primary sources.

First, she was Southeast Asian. In this group, her credentials to speak about the Southeast Asian community, or about racism, might readily have been accepted. The participant's comment that he had not come for a session on racism relates not only to the committee member's unfortunate introduction but also stems from a pervasive perception that a person of colour only has expertise on racism. But the educator's task was to engage participants in an examination of the media. Broadcast and print media overwhelmingly use white males as spokespersons on most economic, social, and political issues. These images are powerful in shaping our perceptions of who is qualified to speak or lead an examination of the media.

Second, she was a woman. It is not clear if gender dynamics were also at work in the male participant's resistance to her credentials. But this is not uncommon.

Third, she was not a journalist or academic; she was an educator with a knowledge of process and of the impact of media in shaping perception. Her skills and knowledge were not readily identifiable through a list of degrees and media postings: the trappings most people accept as indicators of a media expert.

Fourth, the democratic process she was using was unfamiliar to people schooled in sitting, listening, and writing down information transmitted by "people who know". Many people view with suspicion educators who resist "telling people what they know" and begin with a belief in participant experience and knowledge. (See chapter two, in particular, for our examination of this kind of process.)

In anticipating these difficulties of establishing credibility, this educator had written and reviewed with the committee an appropriate introduction to herself that emphasized what she was bringing to the workshop. She had also fortified herself with some written handouts to reassure those who require print to make certain they are learning.

Finally, in conjunction with the steering committee she had paid particular attention to the development of a design and hoped that the committee, with this additional experience of work with her, would be able to communicate her competence to the rest of the group. This form of democratic planning is necessary not just to establish credibility but also to ensure that the workshop meets the needs of those requesting it.

125

It is also important to remember that members of any group will have different criteria for what makes a person credible. One facilitator may not be able to meet all of these criteria equally well.

Insider/outsider

There are different tensions for the insider and for the outsider in establishing credibility while working democratically. In this case, the educator was an outsider, recommended by one of the steering committee members because of her skills along with her perspective and experience.

She used the planning process to make the rest of the committee familiar with her skills and then relied on the committee to establish her credentials with the participants. It is important that insiders who solicit outsiders to assist in their learning take responsibility for welcoming and confirming the abilities of the outsider to do so; and share the responsibility and the heat (when necessary) for the process.

Participant Expectations

Without belabouring the obvious, if participants attend a workshop thinking it will be one thing, and the facilitator offers something radically different, there will be trouble.

In this case the educator had tried to reconcile participants' expectations with the design developed with the steering committee. She did this through the wording of the advance publicity, through a negotiation of objectives at the beginning, and through referring to the objectives when there was resistance.

This approach accomplishes two important things: it establishes joint responsibility for the design of the workshop; and it provides a framework for common agreement. Any objections can be referred back to this agreement. Even so there is always the possibility that the original objectives will have to be revised and the direction shifted.

BARB THOMAS

Experiences of top-down education

All of us have been schooled in undemocratic learning processes. Teachers teach; students learn. Teachers talk; students listen. Teachers know; students don't.

These experiences inform the expectations many people bring to our workshops about who will do what, and how things will happen. Many people are comforted by having an "expert" at the front of the room. They can afford to be passive; they have someone to argue with, but not necessarily to engage with; they can scrutinize the expert and avoid their own location in the issue; and they can be assured that whatever happens they "are learning something" because someone is talking at them. And some experts can make wonderful, engaging presentations that do connect with people's experiences and deepen their understanding. This is not an argument against expertise. This is a challenge to use expertise democratically, so that the expertise of participants is also affirmed and called upon.

Social change education encourages people to identify, value, and contribute what they know so they can solve problems together. The social change educator must design different processes that actively invite such joint learning and problem-solving.

But to do so requires an acknowledgement that this is not familiar terrain to most people. We find that stating objectives, providing clear structures, and making print resources available are strategies that establish credibility but don't, in themselves, confirm the educator as expert.

At the same time, educators do bring particular skills and knowledge to events – otherwise they wouldn't be doing the work. They have to find the appropriate moments to add content that is new to the participants and to challenge strongly held views that are sexist, racist, or class-biased. Social change education is not an invitation for the educator to be self-effacing. It is a challenge to provide expertise strategically and respectfully.

Tips on establishing credibility / sharing the expert role

✦ **Negotiate objectives with participants.** Facilitators should tell participants about the objectives that inform the design. Allow for enough time at the beginning of a session to hear what individual participants want to learn. Talk about how these wants can be met, what shifts can be made to accommodate particular concerns, and what participant goals are not possible in the workshop.

This process establishes that the educator has given previous thought to the workshop and signals a readiness to accommodate the particular, unanticipated needs of participants. It also indicates the limits of what the process can provide.

✦ **Acknowledge participants who helped with planning/design.** Crediting the time and insights of participants who helped with planning is a clear statement to other participants that the facilitator thought about their particular needs and drew upon expertise from their own ranks. It can also acknowledge that some of the members, in fact, were responsible for drawing up the objectives of the event.

✦ **Speak to familiar aspects of the organizational culture.** Try to use terminology familiar to participants. For example, with trade unionists, you'd say "course leader" rather than "facilitator". When you use illustrative examples from other contexts, frame them in the organizational language that participants will feel comfortable with. When you are not sure about the language or norms of the group, ask them for help. Draw on what they know best: their own workplace.

✦ **Take time with introductions.** Get participants to introduce themselves, along with the particular interest that brings them to the workshop. If you record these comments on flip-chart paper, participants will see that you've heard them and that you respect their knowledge and their hopes for the workshop. If people resist, saying that they know each other already, throw in some surprising or obscure questions (place of birth, number of brothers or sisters) to make sure that they learn something new about each other. (And remember the various activities for getting started outlined in chapter three.)

✦ **Link the print materials you have brought to the discussion.** Ironically, many people who are reassured by the provision of print material do not read it. But they often do read materials after a stimulating, challenging workshop. The use of print material reinforces a facilitator's knowledge of the subject. People are more likely to read it, though, if facilitators link each piece of material to something discussed during the workshop.

✦ **Type up and give back participant notes, when possible.** If you have recorded participant comments, insights, and questions throughout the workshop, try to return this information to the participants. (The recording is best done on flip-chart paper or blackboard so participants can see what they are producing.)

Returning participants' knowledge to them accomplishes three things: it documents the workshop and what it produced and makes this information available for future use by facilitators and participants; it confirms and values for participants what they know and have produced; and it provides an occasion to have further contact with participants following a workshop. (See chapter two for more detailed suggestions about the process of documenting the event.)

GIVING AND GETTING FEEDBACK

A Story

Some twenty women who work in shelters for abused women are participating in a five-day, facilitator-training program. On the fourth day, working in small teams, they design their own workshops and are about to begin practising facilitation. The purpose of the exercise is not only to strengthen facilitation skills but also, following each team's presentation, to practise giving each other supportive, critical feedback.

In preparation for the activity the facilitator helps participants develop rules for feedback. She asks them, "What behaviours help you to hear people's criticisms as useful and not attacking?"

The participants generate a list of guidelines they'll use to critique each other's work. Among other things, they agree that each woman should indicate one thing she likes and one thing she thinks can be improved; that they should all speak for themselves and not universalize their comments; and that comments be specific, not general.

During the feedback after each team's presentation, two women continually interrupt and violate their own guidelines. They launch immediately into criticisms of what was wrong with the team's presentation, without mentioning anything positive. They make comments such as, "Nobody could understand your instructions," implying that the others agree with what they are saying. The facilitator continues to stop the process and question their behaviour in light of the guidelines.

Later, in the evaluation of the session, the two women reflect critically on their own inability to follow feedback guidelines. They name this as a significant problem in their own political organizations. The result, they conclude, is that people stop listening to each other and instead spend energy defending and attacking. Critical feedback becomes a way of hurting others and not building the work.

So what's going on?

Most people think of criticism as negative, and three important social factors encourage this notion.

The first is that in many capitalist societies people are trained to view criticism as having meaning only at a personal level – and not at a collective level. Critical comments, then, become one person's response to another person's skills, knowledge, and understanding. People don't see these comments as an opportunity for everyone to learn something both for themselves and for their joint efforts.

On the other hand, if people adopt a spirit of shared responsibility for learning and action, this step would not only promote more shared ownership of a problem but also help establish a way of developing useful approaches to addressing the problem.

Second, there's a standard response to this personalization of criticism, which is not to give it at all for fear of hurting the person's feelings. It's not uncommon for people to say publicly what they like and privately, to someone else, what they dislike. This produces dishonesty and distrust in groups, and

129

prevents potentially helpful insights from informing the collective analysis and action of the group.

Third, in organizations that view themselves as oppositional and action-oriented, a culture of criticism often develops that ignores personal feelings. Instead, the strategy and the work are deemed important. Despite persistent evidence to the contrary, personal feelings are viewed as a liberal luxury. This results in the suppression of hurt, anxiety, and anger and helps to produce ways of talking that are, in fact, competitive, aggressive, and non-collaborative.

These processes also suppress more kindly emotions, such as approval or affirmation. A tendency builds up to reduce all differences to political tensions, even in situations where differences in social identity and organizational role may be significant.

A central task of social change education is to develop skills in constructive, critical dialogue. These skills include abilities to:

◇ raise questions for clarification
◇ probe for the reasons for a statement or action
◇ identify and name one's own personal responses to someone's actions or work, whether in accord with or in challenge to that work
◇ suggest alternative approaches.

The development of these skills must be planned and deliberate. If, for instance, you build in ongoing evaluation throughout the event you will be providing early opportunities for participants to give critical feedback, which can be used to make changes immediately. This strategy influences the quality of the critical analysis; helps to break down the barriers between educators and participants; encourages collective ownership of the process; and makes participants more ready to take risks, knowing they can survive the critical feedback – that they can, in fact, be stimulated by it.

Building on curious and open responses to criticism will encourage participants to be more constructively frank with each other. This in turn builds a spirit of inquiry and trust. Participants will understand that criticism is designed to strengthen people and their work, and not to belittle or demean them.

Tips on giving and getting feedback

A strategy we've used in many skillshops with educators is to develop guidelines for feedback. The following tips draw on participants' own lists from such sessions and can be used by facilitators and participants alike.

✦ **Talk in the first person.** Statements such as "I felt ..." or "When I heard you say ..." communicate personal responsibility for responses. They do not claim, nor should they, to speak for others.

✦ **Be specific.** Statements such as "When you said this, I ..." or "Your idea about ..." focus on the particular action or statement. These statements bring the discussion close to home, make it easier to examine and tackle. Avoid comments such as "You keep ..." or "You always...".

◆ **Challenge the idea or action, not the person.** It doesn't help to draw attention to the pitch of someone's voice or a stutter. Stick to actions or behaviours that a person can modify (if they agree this would be useful).

◆ **Combine recognition of what worked with a challenge to improve.** Few people are so thick-skinned that they do not need acknowledgement of their achievements. Providing this recognition helps to situate suggestions and challenges in a context of effort and accomplishment. It helps a person hear the spirit of a positive criticism.

Again, be as specific as possible. For example, if a person sounds preachy in a part of the presentation but engages people in a lively way in another part, refer to the positive side as a specific model of tone, strategy, and style.

Explore what makes something work. Although successes are not accidents, they aren't as noticeable as problems. Uncovering the thoughts and skills behind a success can be instructive.

◆ **Ask questions to clarify or probe reasons.** Questions such as "What did you take into account when you decided . . .?" or "What did you mean when you said . . .?" credits the person with selection and judgement. The questions also help avoid criticisms and suggestions that miss the mark and are irrelevant to what the person is trying to do.

◆ **Identify the bridges.** When you are giving critical feedback to a participant, remind her or him of what you have in common. Comments such as "I know that when we do X we tend to . . ." remind the person that you're on the same side. Sometimes a part of this same bridge may be to acknowledge differences. For example, "As a man, my experience is a bit different, but . . .".

◆ **Acknowledge how you connect to a problem.** Because people can learn as much from what goes badly as from what goes well, it helps to show how you have also experienced a thorny problem. Statements such as "I've had this problem, myself, too" or "This is helpful for me / us to think about because . . ." emphasize that this is not just an academic exercise for you as facilitator.

◆ **Wherever possible, make suggestions for alternative approaches.** Questions such as "Have you considered . . .?" or "What would happen if we tried . . .?" open a range of possible different responses. The use of "we" suggests that the issue and its solution is of interest to the whole group. Encourage others to add to the generation of different options. This will make it clear that there is not just one other (and therefore better) way to do it.

◆ **Don't assume that a difference is political.** Check to see whether a conflict is based on different experience, different social identity, or a different role in the organization. The response may clarify the extent to which debate can change a person's view and ascertain how important a view is to that person's self-image.

CHALLENGING
AND
ENCOURAGING
RESISTANCE

A story

A union educator is teaching a group of shop stewards how to teach other shop stewards. As they examine the grievance procedure, one participant asks if the educator knows how many steps there are in the procedure. The educator say he doesn't know about this particular collective agreement, and he asks if anyone else in the group knows. The participant, a little irritated, asks the educator what he's doing teaching the course if he doesn't know something so basic.

The other shop stewards shift about anxiously and look expectantly at the educator. "What I know," he says, "is how to teach. I don't know about your collective agreement. If you know enough about teaching to teach this course tomorrow, then I'll go out and watch some movies and you can take over". He suggests they take a break and then come back and talk about it some more, if they need to.

After the break the participant comes over to the educator and says, "I'm ready to deal, on the basis that when we're talking about grievances, we talk. When we're talking teaching approaches, you talk."

"It won't work just like that," the educator says, " but it's a good start. We need each other to do the job. We can use each other's knowledge."

At the end of the day the "resister" approaches the educator again. He says, "It's good you stopped me when you did. It's not nice to say, but I would have pushed you out of the room."

So what's going on?

In this case the resister is operating from a set of beliefs about teaching and learning. Teachers should know a proscribed body of knowledge, and if they don't know, they shouldn't teach.

What's hidden, perhaps even from the holder of this perspective, are the answers to questions such as: "Who decided what was important to know? Why doesn't participant knowledge carry the same weight as teacher knowledge? How do such notions of knowledge reinforce dependency in participants and power in facilitators?

In liberal adult education literature, resisters are people to be managed, suppressed, and brought on side. But a central purpose of social change education is to build resisters. (That said, we may often wish that they would develop and act out their resistance in someone else's program.) Facilitators have a dual task: to defend a program against sabotage; and to use resistance as a source of energy and potential insight in a group.

Resistance as sabotage

In this case the facilitator acknowledged the resister's question and sought an answer from participants. The resister's belief framework then moved him from an interest in the answer to a challenge to the facilitator's credibility.

The facilitator stood his ground on what he knew and what he didn't know and challenged the resister to consider this situation. He defended the program against sabotage. At the same time he encouraged the resister to reflect on the premises of his statement.

Resistance as creative moment

A further step is to use the incident, consciously, with the group. The facilitator could stop the session or perhaps, at a later point, ask participants if they ever have times in their education work when they don't know something. What do they do? What's the cost of pretending to know?

He could also ask: How do they use what participants know? What is the impact of drawing on the knowledge of participants? What is the impact if the facilitator always knows or appears to know? What behaviour on the part of the facilitator helps participants to value what they, themselves, know?

Resistance as information

Facilitators have a responsibility to look at resistance as a source of important information, of content for group learning.

Using resistance creatively for information depends on our assessment of where it's coming from. We have found five factors that it's useful to consider as a framework for thinking about this question. While they are posed here as discrete considerations, they often overlap.

BARB THOMAS

133

✦ **First, resistance can stem from a person's social identity and relation to power.**

For example, a man's resistance in a discussion of gender inequity may stem from feelings of guilt or anxiety (among other things). A woman's resistance in the same discussion may result from a desire to be accepted, a fear of being pinpointed, or a fear of losing small gains. For men and women the stakes in gender equity are different. The behaviour resulting from such feelings requires balanced attention to prevent the program from being capsized. At the same time the resistance can be used to clarify different stakes and different relations to power.

✦ **Second, resistance can result from discomfort with the content and perspective.** Participants may find the ideas too alien and the implications for their own lives too threatening. Conversely, people may be critical because the perspective is not challenging enough.

In either case the resistance gives facilitators information about participant responses to their assumptions or tone, or about participant readiness to engage with the issues. Facilitators can see resistance as a strong form of feedback that may signal a problem being experienced by more than one person.

✦ **Third, resistance can be about the process.** A democratic process that values the contributions of all participants takes more time than the delivery of a lecture.

Most people with little experience of the power of such a process frequently become impatient and frustrated. In the union case here the participant was resisting the facilitator's democratic use of the group's knowledge.

✦ **Fourth, resistance can arise from participants' fear about losing their jobs, and a distrust of organizational practices.** For example, in discussions about employment equity many White male employees are afraid that their jobs are on the line – fears that are fuelled by the arbitrary, past practices of management.

✦ **Fifth, "resistance" can arise from critical thinking.** As social change educators, we need to guard against hearing criticism as sabotage. Democratic practice requires not only the ability to hear and disagree but also constant attention to what we might have overlooked.

**Tips on challenging
and encouraging
resistance**

✦ **Smoke out the real agenda.** Pose questions that require resisters to clarify what they mean and what they want.

Often, what people don't say or what they signal non-verbally is what they mean. Make sure you're not spending time on diversions to the real point. When possible, refer back to a participant's earlier comments and actions so you can comment on consistencies or discrepancies.

✦ **Give people the benefit of the doubt, initially.** Social change education demands a belief that people can and want to do the right thing. This does not mean succumbing to naivety. But it does mean taking time to flesh out the experiences and sources of information that have informed an opinion.

✦ **Confront the issues.** Summarize what you hear the person saying. Encourage other participants to get involved. If no one feels able, don't back off. Use the facts and resources you have available. Pose questions that probe the resister's position. Know where you stand on the issue and explain what you are doing and why you are doing it.

✦ **Don't belittle the resister.** Even if the person is behaving in a destructive manner, stick with her or his statements and behaviour. If you counterattack, participants may close ranks against you even if they tend to agree with you. Besides, you would be violating your own principles.

✦ **Ask other participants for their responses.** If one person has had ample time to vent opinions or feelings, and you think those views are not shared by the group, ask if others share them. This deflects things from becoming a two-way conversation between facilitator and resister. It also encourages the group to take responsibility for the time they spend. (This can be a tricky situation, especially if resistance occurs while you are just getting to know participants, or if the situation is particularly volatile.)

✦ **Be prepared to shift and adapt if this is required.** Most resistance is not sabotage. If several people have concerns about moving on before a particular issue is explored more fully, propose a shift of plans to the group, so you can accommodate the anxieties or concerns you are hearing. Encouraging thoughtful resistance means that it be taken seriously and that it informs the process.

✦ **Use Resistance for new insights.** If you can, relate the resistance (as a kind of case study) to a larger issue the group is examining. Encourage people to derive new insights from what was said, and how it was said.

✦ **Know when to move on.** At some point you may have to agree to disagree. It helps, though, to restate the different positions, summarizing where there is agreement and disagreement. Then you have to agree on a process for moving on. First you may have to take a break.

If a person is obstinate and argumentative, you may have to exercise authority to move on. Be sure you have the support of at least three-quarters of the group before doing so, and then you can exercise that authority in the name of the group.

135

WORKING WITH
DISCOMFORT

A story

Two facilitators, one Black, one White, are running an anti-racist facilitator-train-ing program with twenty staff in a social service agency. Half the participants are Black and half White.

By the time the group is part-way through the program, many questions and feelings have arisen, and they all require discussion. The facilitators decide to use one session to talk in two "race-specific" groups, one for Black participants, one for White, with facilitators working in their own racial group.

The group of Black participants has a lengthy discussion about the experience of being Black in Canada and the impact of racism on lives and work. Most of them agree that Black people have no choice but to be anti-racist because as profession-als, as parents, as individuals, their whole lives are conditioned by racism.

One participant disagrees. She says she has never experienced racism in Canada. The others express disbelief but the dissenting participant persists. She says that Black people cause many of their own problems, and that they just have to demonstrate more confidence and they'll be fine. She sees racism as an occa-sional problem caused by ignorant behaviour.

The facilitator asks about where and how she has developed her confidence, and there's a discussion about class background and privilege and about the impact these factors have on responses to racism in Canada. Many in the group are not comfortable with the discussion and several of them keep returning to stories in which White people behave in deplorable ways. Some group members also disagree about what parts of the discussion can usefully be reported back to the large group that includes White participants.

Finally the facilitator leans forward and asks, "You've all been talking about White people as though they're the only ones with any influence. What about us? What do we influence?"

There is silence. The facilitator waits. Then one participant says, "It's some-times easier to talk about Whites than it is to talk about the things that divide us. The greater evil is White racism. It also influences the divisions between us."

The facilitator answers by saying, "Let's acknowledge that there are as many differences between us as there are between Whites. And we've been exploring some of these areas of disagreement." Participants nod.

The facilitator continues. "But there are three areas of real discomfort that it seems necessary to discuss if we are to be able to act together. One is the experi-ence of privilege in our own backgrounds that makes us hesitate to take the risks we know are needed. A second is to concentrate on what we can influence, regard-less of what White people do. The third is the degree of candour with which we share this discussion with the White participants. Do you see this as useful dis-cussion? If so, should I record our comments?" Again, the participants nod.

In the time remaining the group tackles the questions of what they could influ-ence and what conditions would help them take the risks involved.

So what's going on?   Discomfort is, for better or worse, an integral part of social change education. It occurs when questions of social identity, oppression, and action have an impact on a personal level. That is, it happens when discussion is no longer focused out there on "those people" but in here on us and me, and on what we are and are not doing about it.

We want to consider three factors that influence how facilitators work with discomfort: the facilitator's own stakes; the dynamics of the group; the costs of not working with the discomfort.

The facilitator's stakes

In this case the facilitator was able to relate, as a Black person, to the issues causing discomfort. She knew what they were about. She could use the pronoun "we". The group trusted her as a Black person and as a skilled facilitator. She used both these identities in her work with the group.

But this identification is not without its problems. As a Black activist she might disagree with the position of the dissenting participant who said she had no experience with racism. In this case the facilitator used her experience as a Black person only to inform her questions about confidence and privilege. At the same time, she had to play her role as facilitator and avoid taking sides. And she had to encourage supportive challenge to this participant from the other participants.

She also used her experience both as a Black activist and a skilled facilitator to name the discomfort evident in the group. But again, she had to stick to a facilitator role in drawing out the discussion and to make sure she didn't become enmeshed in her own Black activist role.

In this case she did share the relevant social identities, of race and class. She was an insider, not to the organization, but to the subject and general experience of it. And she was an educator/activist. The facilitator's stakes vary from situation to situation, but they are usually shaped by these three factors.

It is also true that our positions and discomforts change over time. To work effectively with discomfort, it is essential that we bring along our own clarity on our current stances and areas of unease, as well as on our appropriate roles.

Dynamics of the group

This case suggests four factors that we need to consider in assessing whether group dynamics provide positive conditions for probing discomfort.

First, most members of the group actively wanted to gain more knowledge and work towards informed action. There was general agreement, with one exception, on the role of racism in shaping people's lives and work. This agreement and commitment to act are an important precondition for securing permission to probe discomfort. If the group had been divided more evenly on this, or if it had been in general agreement with the dissenter, the issues would have been different. This facilitator was able to use discomfort as a catalyst to discuss the less comfortable aspects of class identification. In this way, discomfort became a resource.

137

A second factor was that group members had worked together with their white colleagues before this session. They had begun to develop a sense of themselves as a group, and they had enough trust to disclose more and examine those disclosures together.

Third, the group trusted the facilitator. They had observed and worked with her during the first part of the program and knew her principled, skilled leadership.

Finally, the group had the time to examine the discomfort and work with it, both during this session, and in sessions to come. Learning often happens as discomfort gets slowly digested, and people have different ways of working this through.

Costs of not working with discomfort

When they assess whether to name and work with discomfort at a given moment, facilitators must think about the costs of not doing so. In this case the discomfort was a running current in the discussion and had been avoided and unnamed.

If the facilitator had not challenged the discomfort, chances are the group would have continued to avoid these questions, which touched them so personally. But the unease would have surfaced sporadically in other ways. If this kind of unease is not named, the sporadic emissions become almost impossible to address.

RICK ARNOLD

In most groups there is both a fear that the discomfort will be named, and a great unease when it is not. People sometimes avoid the problem, because they can't quite pinpoint what's going on; or they avoid it because they don't trust the group and fear disclosure and attack. Whatever the reason, avoidance is not a healthy basis for social change education and action.

The primary agenda, in this particular case, cannot be met without addressing the secondary agenda, which is usually something like, "Where am I in this, and what's really stopping me from getting anywhere?"

Finally, activists who must take an oppositional stance and/or are part of oppressed groups have a common tendency to concentrate on publicly radical positions and avoid the mess in their own yard. This tendency can have direct implications for the way they treat each other, the honesty they bring to helping others learn and act, and the climate of trust in organizations doing social change work.

To help work through this problem, certain questions might be posed: What conditions need to be created to enable us to work with discomfort? Whose feelings are being hurt in the suppression of frank discussion? Whose feelings will be hurt in frank discussion? And what steps should be taken to address these emotions more satisfactorily?

Social change education has a responsibility to work with discomfort – not just to create a productive workshop but to improve the strength, trust, climate, and viability of the organizations working for social justice.

Tips on working with discomfort

✦ **Watch for the symptoms.** Silence, shuffling, frequent breaks, side conversations, repeated returns to more comfortable terrain, personal attacks: these are all signals of discomfort in a group. Facilitators must also watch for what people are avoiding and for when avoiding behaviour occurs, in order to name it accurately.

✦ **Name what you think it is.** In the case here, the facilitator was able to put words to what she saw. In some cases, it may be more appropriate to ask people about how they felt doing a particular activity, or about how they feel discussing a particular issue. This provides a space for participants to name for themselves what is going on.

✦ **Probe what people say they mean.** If participants say something vague and seem to be inferring something quite stronger, ask what they mean. "Say some more about that." "Do you mean this, or that?" "Are you saying that ...?" "You seem to be saying this, but earlier you referred to that. Is it hard for you to talk about ...?"

These are all ways in which facilitators demonstrate listening behaviour and at the same time challenge participants to say what is really on their minds.

✦ **Don't be afraid of silence.** Don't fill in all the spaces. Let people sit and listen to the question or statement posed. Often it takes people time to find the words or the courage to say the words.

✦ **Give support to talk about feelings.** No, you are not running a therapy group. But social justice work must be fuelled by feelings – anger, hope, love, fear, passion – or it becomes a very hollow affair. There is a place for analysis, a place for making statements, a place for action. There must also be a place for sharing who we are and how we feel about what we do. Discomfort usually resides in these feelings. The tips in this section suggest some ways to bring the feelings out into the open and to validate them.

✦ **Ask permission to pursue discomfort.** There is no point in probing discomfort if the group doesn't want to do so. Name what you think is going on, or get participants to do so, then acknowledge that this is a different way of dealing with the agenda than planned and ask if the group finds this process useful. (Facilitators have to exercise judgement to assess the appropriate moment for intervening in this way.)

✦ **Record what people say.** This, of course, is again subject to the group's permission. But writing comments on flip-chart paper helps the group focus visually as well as aurally on the task, helps members build on, refer to, and develop each other's insights, and helps them see common ground as well as disagreement in the group.

✦ **Ensure there will be time to heal.** Don't initiate this kind of process in the last five minutes of a session or at the very end of a program. People need to be able to come back together after thinking about the discussion. They can then pursue the issues further or refer to them in their continuing work together.

✦ **Encourage participant contributions.** Often participants offer a hand, an insight, a question that shifts the frame and signals equal responsibility for the process. The educator should be alert to such overtures and encourage them.

✦ **Know when to move on.** You can sense when the group has worked with a discussion of discomfort as far as it can. People start repeating themselves or introducing other subjects. The tense energy that informs talk of discomfort dissipates. When this happens, summarize the main points and suggest that participants take these things into account as they proceed with the original agenda.

CONFLICT:
HEADING INTO
THE WIND

A story

A three-day conference on coalition-building brings together two hundred seasoned educators and organizers from a variety of different sectors: aboriginal peoples, women, anti-poverty and anti-racist groups, unions, and others. The organizers have asked the facilitators to help design a participatory process for each small group, with a view to emerging with recommendations for coalition-building.

One workshop group, with twenty-eight participants speaking both English and French, sees substantial differences emerging by lunch of the first day.

The facilitators had allocated the entire morning to activities that encouraged discussion of identity and experience in activist work. They based this design on the assumption that the participants needed to know and trust the others in the room before a discussion of coalition strategy could work effectively.

Shortly before lunch a couple of White men in the group express impatience. This friendly chitchat is all very well, they say. But there's an urgency to respond to the reactionary initiatives of corporations and government. The discussion should be focusing on building unity and making a real challenge to the strengthening conservative agenda. "Let's get on with the real discussion," one of the two men says.

An aboriginal man vehemently disagrees. "It's premature and dangerous to move to strategy before trust is built," he says. "And building trust requires a deeper understanding of Native issues than this discussion has shown so far. It's time White people started listening to us."

These turn out to be the last comments before participants break for lunch, and the two facilitators are left to figure out what to do next. They quickly come up with a post-lunch activity and sketch out a possible revised agenda.

When participants return, the facilitators restate the two opposing positions, which they call "Action Now" and "Time to Listen". They ask one spokesperson for each to go stand at opposite ends of the room, leaving space at either end for more extreme positions. They ask the rest of the participants to physically place themselves in relation to these two people/positions.

Three participants join "Action Now", all from western Canada; five people join "Time to Listen", most of them from Quebec; three clusters develop somewhere in the middle. The facilitators ask the participants in these five clusters to talk to each other about why they are there. Some reshuffling happens as a result. After this a spokesperson from each of the five clusters states her or his group's views to the whole group.

The facilitators propose a revised agenda and indicate how each cluster's concerns could be met by a few further amendments. The group accepts this new agenda by consensus and the plan works well as a framework for the rest of the workshop program.

141

So what's going on?   Conflict will always be a feature of discussions of oppression and social action. In this case the tension appeared to be about how to spend the time available to the workshop. But these "differences of opinion" were also intimately connected to two important factors emanating from outside the walls of the workshop: unequal experiences of power based on race; and different strategies for activist work based on different analysis.

People tend to think and act based on a number of factors: their own experiences of society; the "logic" of the culture of their organizations and/or communities; and their individual inclinations. In this case the people holding different positions are all operating from an experience of and commitment to social justice. This is common ground. Participants should always be reminded, in moments of conflict, of this common ground.

Often, when you use the tension of the moment creatively the results can be more powerful than you had planned. You can only handle this process if you are clear on where you want to go and what you can drop. Paradoxically, you're more able to wing it if you're well prepared.

Power relations, respecting difference, developing ways to work together: these are the issues in social change education. In such cases a respectful and clear grappling with conflict is an important aspect of democratic practice. Participants can learn much from how they acknowledge and embrace conflict as part of learning. They can also take this learning back to their own political work.

After considering what had happened, the facilitators in this case felt they had stopped the process at the right time. Highlighting the conflict early rather than suppressing it was the key factor in the success of the workshop as a whole. Suppression would have only produced conflict later when there was no time left to address it.

Conflict can stem from a different language for talking about the same things. It can stem from an inability to listen and to hear experiences, frameworks, patterns of speech different from your own. So the facilitators' roles can include questioning, checking, challenging, and summarizing until the group reaches a certain clarity on how positions are similar and different.

ALOK MUKHERJEE

EDUCATING FOR A CHANGE

Tips on handling conflict

✦ **Plan for conflict about one-third of the way along.** Conflict will occur: it should be a part of the learning that takes place throughout an educational event. But participants usually start politely and carefully, which means that facilitators have to dig up earlier rather than later what's under the surface. Doing this allows time for a full discussion and further work. In our experience this stage often comes in the second day of a four- or five-day course.

✦ **Stop the process when conflict seems to be building up consistently.** Not all conflict is significant. But when it builds up it will sabotage the process. It's better as a facilitator to show conscious leadership and incorporate the conflict into everyone's learning.

✦ **Name opposing positions as clearly as possible.** Facilitators should highlight the key elements of the conflict as they hear it, allowing participants to clarify or elaborate. This allows everyone to proceed in the discussion as cleanly as possible.

✦ **Explore the whys as well as the whats of people's positions.** All participants should look critically at the sources of conflict as well as try to understand the experiences that have informed differing positions. Exploring the whys also affords a chance to assess how deeply held an opinion is, and whether there are new considerations that can influence it. Role-play is a useful tool for this kind of probing process.

✦ **Where possible, use conflict to illuminate larger social issues.** Invite participants to consider the group conflict as an example or case study of a form of larger inequity or domination. For example, in the case here the conflict in the group mirrored larger differences and concerns raised by aboriginal peoples at the conference itself.

✦ **Encourage participant responsibility for process.** Facilitators can lead a group in surfacing and guiding a process for addressing the conflict. But this process should not result in a limited dialogue between a facilitator and one or two participants. Participants know when they are no longer benefiting from what is going on. The facilitator can check with all participants – their energy levels, the time they want to take up – and get suggestions about approaches for moving on. A round robin can be a useful way to gain knowledge of the individual learning that comes out of a difficult situation.

✦ **Seek agreement on a way to proceed, not on the positions.** When opinions are firmly held and loudly stated, easy agreement is unlikely. So facilitators should only try to summarize the different positions. Seek agreement on a way to proceed that both acknowledges the differences and draws on a common interest to benefit from the workshop.

TIMING: EXIT
LINES

A story

The final half hour of a workshop with community workers speeds by. Participants had been examining approaches to addressing conflict in their organizations. Four small groups, each with a different scenario, had prepared dramatizations that posed possible strategies. After each drama the large group would then suggest and practise a variety of ways to approach the problem.

It took longer than usual for the groups to prepare their dramas and now, with five minutes to go, one group still hasn't presented its play. The facilitator asks everyone if they can stay for another half-hour. Some people nod, but a few say no. One woman, clutching her purse, gets up apologetically to say that she has to take her child to the doctor. Two others say that their street parking will expire in a few minutes so they'll have to leave. There is a general murmuring and gathering up of papers.

The facilitator, now with two minutes left, apologizes to the fourth group, telling them there isn't going to be time for their presentation. He suggests that maybe they can use it at some other time in their organization. Some group members look relieved, others annoyed.

The facilitator, speaking very quickly, begins summarizing what they had accomplished during the day. The two participants with parking problems get up, looking regretful, to go move their cars. A couple of participants are exchanging addresses and phone numbers for a future get-together. A couple of other people exchange last-minute words with the two people with over-parked cars.

At four o'clock the facilitator says to the group, "I know you have to leave. I'm sorry we were so rushed in the end. The work you did, and the insights you brought, really generated some wonderful ideas for addressing conflict. I hope you find you can use them in your work."

A few people clap, a few people gather up their papers, a couple of others remain deep in conversation.

So what's going on?

We have all had this all-too-familiar experience. You can have a good design, lots of participant energy, new insights, but none of it compensates for bad timing. In this case, bad timing is responsible for three unwanted conditions at the end of the workshop.

Unequal treatment of participants

Four small groups had prepared dramatizations, but only three of them got the chance to present their work. By the time the facilitator acknowledged the time problem, it was too late to do anything but apologize and quickly close the workshop.

In addition, the last-minute nature of the closure meant that only a few people paid attention to the wrap-up. The rest had moved on to their personal affairs.

No evaluation of learning by participants

Five minutes is not enough to shift the design, find out who can stay, summarize what's been done, and elicit participant responses to the day. It takes a good half-hour in a day-long workshop for a facilitator to lead participants through a reflection on the day's work and the learnings that have emerged. This time gets even more compressed if the participants also have to stop and think about the next steps they want to take together as a group.

This is a crucial, often overlooked piece of the work. People frequently have difficulty naming what they have learned. They usually need ample time for both individual and collective discussion to help bring new insights to the surface and to consider how they will use them.

No closure on the group's work together

A shared experience of working together requires closure – an acknowledgement of what participants have learned from each other, a time to say good-bye. In this case, a few people were taking care of that informally, with whispered conversations to others who were leaving, or by exchanging phone numbers.

Tips on timing

✦ **Don't plan more than three full activities for a day.** Chapter two, on design, has more about this. When your design starts to feel complicated, it's usually a sign that your timing will be in trouble.

✦ **Mark times to begin and end activities on your design notes.** This provides a guide for where you should be when. When an activity takes less or more time, you can shift accordingly as you go.

✦ **Negotiate time from the beginning of the workshop.** One of the starting points of the day is confirming times for breaks, lunch, and ending. It is important to stick to the times negotiated with participants.

✦ **Cut from the middle, not from the beginning or the end.** Introductions and establishing the climate and process of the workshop take approximately half an hour, depending on the length of the workshop. (See chapter two on starting points.) Evaluation and closure take another half-hour at the end.

In the case above, the facilitator should have recognized by early afternoon that he was behind schedule. He could have negotiated with the group about having only two dramatizations presented and given the other two groups observer roles. Or he could have run all four dramatizations back to back without the follow-up discussions, stopping after each one only to summarize the nature of the conflict. Then, after all the dramas had been done, the group could have chosen one to focus attention on.

These are some of the ways that you can alter timing on your feet while at the same time sticking to the objectives and rudiments of your design.

✦ **Cut the amount of data generated and processed.** If you are behind time, simplify the task of the small groups or limit the amount of small-group discussion reported to the large group.

✦ **Negotiate shifts in plans with participants.** This is not necessary when participants are not affected by the change. But in the case above, the time it took participants to prepare their dramas in small groups was extended. When facilitators notice this sort of thing happening they can do a number of things. They can indicate the time problem and suggest that the presentation of each small group be confined to a certain number of minutes. They can ask if there are groups who particularly want to make presentations and others who don't mind forgoing theirs. Or they can divide participants in half, so two groups present their dramas to each other.

If the dramatizations themselves go way over time, facilitators can, at least half an hour before the workshop's planned ending, make a proposal to spend the remaining time summarizing learning. If they do this, they must clear the change with any groups who have not presented.

✦ **Negotiate, when unanticipated issues arise.** Often an activity generates important discussion, conflict, or discomfort that a facilitator can't anticipate. When this happens the facilitator can share the responsibility for timing with the group, making a comment such as "We have spent fifteen minutes on this now, and it seems that we are not finished. Are people agreed that this is important to pursue? If so, we'll have to cut back on the dramatizations."

RICK ARNOLD

DEBORAH BARNDT

147

THE
FACILITATOR'S
ROLE

In brief, a facilitator is responsible for working effectively with a group to help reach the objectives for an event. To do this, a facilitator must

◇ watch the time and make sure that pacing is appropriate to the group
◇ encourage the active participation of all group members
◇ acknowledge and draw upon differences within the group
◇ encourage the precise and frank naming of issues
◇ draw on the range of knowledge and experience in the group
◇ offer information, frameworks, and insights when appropriate
◇ summarize what's been accomplished at strategic points during the session
◇ constructively address conflict and discomfort
◇ work democratically, with the space, resources, time, and people in the room
◇ encourage critical questions and problem posing
◇ consciously build a spirit of collective as well as individual inquiry and will to act.

Social change facilitators must push beyond the limits of liberal adult education

◇ in the questions and problems they pose
◇ in the ways they engage intellect, emotions, and creativity
◇ in the conceptual connections they encourage
◇ in the democratic relations they establish between learners and facilitator
◇ in the explicitly political task they undertake as educators
◇ in the constant self-assessment of stakes, commitment, risks, and tolerance of ambiguity that this work requires.

In framing this discussion around the eight arenas of facilitator work – using space, making the most of who we are, establishing credibility and sharing the expert role, giving and getting feedback, encouraging/challenging resistance, working with discomfort, addressing conflict, and timing – we have tried not only to place the role of facilitator into a working context but also to make it inclusive of different sectors, issues, and objectives. We also wanted the cases, cumulatively, to celebrate and speak to the range of social change education in which we and our readers are engaged.

At the same time we are aware that these cases are limited. They are only examples and we haven't been able to provide examples of the issues and dynamics facing differently abled people, poor people, or older people in workshop situations. This speaks to gaps in our own knowledge and experience. We hope that the other people in our network and wider educational community who work with different sectors will take this as an invitation to use what is helpful here – and to find opportunities to share what they know with us.

5

Looking Back:

Issues Emerging from our Practice

6 LOOKING FORWARD: Implications for our work in the 1990's

5 LOOKING BACK: Issues emerging from our practice

3 SHAPING OUR TOOLS: Developing and Using Activities

2 WORKING BY DESIGN: Putting together a program

4 WORKING ON OUR FEET: The practice of democratic facilitation

1 THIS IS OUR CHANCE: Educating Strategically

Speaking at a race-relations conference in March 1989 about the place of aboriginal knowledge in building a future, Professor Marlene Brant Castellano of Trent University stated:

> *Indigenous knowledge is seen to be personal knowledge, in that elders, who carry particular responsibility for teaching the younger generation, do not claim to define an objective reality. They share, rather, what they have seen or validated in their own experience. Knowledge is expressed as perception, derived from a particular perspective, rather than as concept, to which general validity is attributed.... When knowledge is utilized as a basis for community action, it is subject to collective analysis and revision, a process referred to in an oral tradition as "putting our minds together."*

Brant Castellano's explanation of aboriginal knowledge contains many elements in common with our orientation to education for social change. Specifically, we believe that what each of us learn is grounded in our experience and, as such, is laden with the values that ultimately influence how we perceive and give meaning to situations. And the extent to which education can produce community action is the extent to which we all use our collective experiences, analysis, and perceptions.

Education, then, is not objective. It is not value neutral and unitary. Moreover, the action that arises from education cannot be based on the insights and analysis of one individual. Instead, action to transform society must emerge from the collective insights and experiences of everyone in the group or community.

Also, according to an African theologian Emmanuel Tehindrazanarivelo, the African tradition sees education as a process of bringing a sense of awareness to people; that is, an awareness of worth, belonging, and responsibility; a sense of tradition, roots, and projection – a sense of being human within a community. The knowledge produced through education provides people with a vision that makes them able to interpret and to be creative so they can produce action as an expression of their own life and the life of the community.

These principles of education underscore our practice as social change educators. In this chapter, beginning with the assumptions and challenges that form the basis of our practice, we will examine the power relations inherent in learning situations. We will also consider the question of how we might increase our impact on the processes of social change. And we will assess what we have learned about ourselves as educators in the course of our work.

This chapter, unlike the others, draws primarily on examples of our work in the formal education system. We hope this will also help to underline the important role that we think teachers in the classroom can play in social change education.

MARK HENDERSON

THE BASIS OF
OUR PRACTICE

As social change educators we have to acknowledge the assumptions and objectives of our practice so we can confront the issues and challenges that surface as we carry out our work. To do this we must be clear about why we're engaged in social change education, in whose interest we work, how we engage learners in the process, and our role as consultants.

What is education for anyway?

Traditional education is about transferring information that will reproduce values, knowledge, skills, discipline, and occupational capacities that will in turn maintain the present order of society and satisfy people's interest to "fit in".

Social change educators, on the other hand, see education as a way to help people critically evaluate and understand themselves and the world around them, to see themselves as active participants in that world. Our hopes for social transformation are ignited as people come to see themselves as creators of culture, history, and an alternative social vision.

In our practice we assume that we have something to share with learners and participants about how to critically analyse the social system. At the same time we acknowledge our own positions in society and the ways that existing social arrangements limit our achievements and aspirations.

We also assume that people readily engage in discussion and actively work to change their situation. In fact, we often find that it's a struggle to get such discussion going. Many people find it difficult to let go of the long-held belief that the world of the status quo rewards them for sheer hard work and compliance.

151

For example, when we are facilitating workshops, running meetings, or leading discussions, the issue of social inequalities of class, race, or gender often surfaces. We find that the people who are themselves most likely to be the targets of discriminatory attitudes and practices are often the very ones who question the existence of racism, sexism, or other prejudice.

In such situations the question is: how do we help people to be critical of the arrangements for inequality in society or in their organizations so they can work for change – yet do so without extinguishing their optimism?

We know about "starting where individuals are at". But starting from where people are at means unravelling what they hold as "given". It means rearranging a seemingly stable sense of how things fit together or, sometimes, contradicting their own interpretation of their own accomplishment. This process will usually meet with resistance. (See chapter four for discussion of how resistance can be used and challenged.)

The challenge becomes how to keep people talking about issues, how to help them see the personal benefits of understanding the situation and working to change it.

BARB THOMAS

What if you're educating for a change?

As educators our purpose is not only to help people critically assess their personal and social situations but also to help them develop their conviction that change is possible. We have to help them see that they have "what it takes" to initiate and bring about change, not just as individuals but as a collective of people sharing similar goals and wishes.

Participants who believe that education is value neutral tend to see any discussion that criticizes current social arrangements as "left-wing", "negative", "not objective", or "too political". Sometimes they see the educators as "more interested in putting forward their own views than in teaching". They see educators who do not question the status quo as being objective, neutral, and having no ideological position. Sometimes participants will point to the race, gender, or social class background of an educator as factors that skew objectivity.

For example, an educator talking to a class of about thirty-five young men and women with participants from various races, ethnicities, and social classes, said, for the sake of discussion, that class, gender, and race are more likely to influence educational and occupational achievement than ability. Not surprisingly in a society priding itself on an equitable educational system, most participants disagreed. Although the educator gave them numerous examples to the contrary, participants held that ability was the sole determinant of achievement, except in cases where women and racial minorities were given preferential treatment in hiring. They specifically cited Blacks as an example of this preferential treatment.

On the question of income as a barrier to educational opportunities, students argued that "OSAP is there", referring to the Ontario Student Assistance Program. They were almost unanimous in saying that the educator was "selective in the references" that he was citing.

Perhaps our task of uncovering the unequal consequences of race, ethnicity, gender, and class would be easier if people came into more contact with educators promoting a critical approach. But this is not the case for most students. A basic challenge for educators for social change is to work against the power of the traditional laissez-faire approach.

Whose agenda?   *A Caribbean-born educator is invited to give a presentation on Caribbean youth to a group of social service workers. The educator focuses the presentation on the historical, economic, political, and social development of the Caribbean.*

He argues that the social workers should see the diversity of Caribbean people: they come from different islands with different colonial histories, economic resources, and numerous races and ethnicities in the population mix. He says there are many varying influences on the youth the social workers would be seeing: age, time and pattern of family immigration to Canada, class background, economic and social situation in Canada, and attitudes such as racism and the resulting discriminatory practices.

The educator emphasizes that it is impossible to talk of any cultural group as if it were monolithic. He concentrates therefore on providing a framework that workers can use to analyse their cases and to develop the necessary strategies appropriate for the individuals they work with.

At the end of the discussion a participant comments that the presentation hasn't been helpful because it didn't give "specifics" about West Indians. The participant mentions another workshop where the resource person, also a Caribbean person, gave a "good description of West Indians, what they are like, and what to expect".

Clearly, in this situation, the presenter and participants hold different assumptions and expectations. Two things are happening here.

✧ There are different assumptions about learning and teaching on the part of participant and facilitator.

✧ There is a kind of dominant cultural voyeurism. An earlier resource person had demanded nothing of participants but had provided information that participants could organize into existing slots: "Caribbean people are...". This other workshop had made no attempt to help participants locate themselves in relation to the issue. The Caribbean person remained an object of scrutiny.

How did the social change educator approach things differently?

✧ He tried to make the participants and the Caribbean peoples equal subjects in the discussion.

✧ He challenged the stereotypes operating in the interaction between the social workers – service providers from the dominant group – and Caribbean people.

As a result, he encountered resistance.

To try and overcome this resistance the presenter could ask participants to imagine they are giving a presentation on Canadians to West Indians. They have one hour. What would they want West Indians to know, what information would not distort who Canadians are? This is an activity that usually helps participants develop a framework they can use to mull over new information about another group.

Another approach – which could be combined with the previous one – is to ask participants to think about what they already "know" about West Indians. This is an important question because it requires participants to become conscious of how they already organize information about certain people.

The assumptions and expectations of participants are based partly on their reasons for participating in the workshop in the first place. For some, these reasons may include a desire to become more sensitive, more informed, more familiar with an issue so they can obtain "how to" information or inform the direction of their actions. Other participants, particularly in more formal educational settings, only want concrete information – "the recipe". They would rather not be bogged down by theory or a new framework for understanding.

As educators, we have to attend to everyone's agenda – not only our own but the agenda of the participants, the sponsoring organization, and the person within the organization who extended the invitation.

All these agendas contribute to what happens or doesn't happen in the situation. To address all these agendas we need to look for common ground.

VALERIE ALIA

Connecting with learners

If we aren't willing to speak in the language of those we wish to involve in our programs, and to use the symbols and images of that language, our reluctance may send out the message that certain groups and people are either not welcome or are being patronized. We will be setting up a barrier.

This barrier may prove a difficult one to break down. It is based on the cultural and class allegiances that inform the traditional approach to education; on the notion that by adopting the language, symbols, and images of "other" groups, our social positions and identities become endangered. But this is a tricky question: sometimes it is also false to adopt the language of other groups, because doing so can be perceived as a form of appropriation, of "going Native".

But just in showing that we have taken the time to learn about and relate to the symbols and images of various cultural and class groupings, we have the potential of lessening social distance. We can establish that these are things we share; these are things that define group membership and identity.

When we try to speak in the other's language, however imperfectly, we communicate powerfully that we accept the other. Symbols and images are more complex, but equally powerful. Everyday behaviour, ordinary forms of interchange, ways of acknowledging ourselves and others: these are all symbolic. Our willingness to recognize these symbols and accept what is intended by them is a way of lessening social distance.

Participants, especially if they are culturally or racially different, are sensitive to how educators display a knowledge and appreciation of their values, life experiences, issues, and concerns. At the same time, while we have to be careful about appearing to be "going Native" or becoming a pseudo-minority, minority status is not a state of mind but lived oppression. We must always remember that privilege remains intact even if we take on the lingo and forms of non-dominant groups.

Educators as consultants: who are they?

Social change educators can play a significant consultative role in helping members of oppressed groups understand their situation in society and act to bring about change if necessary.

For some of us, consulting is a way of life – it's how we earn our rent. So it is appropriate to ask ourselves some questions: Who are the consultants? What are the politics of consulting? What are some of the issues faced by educators who freelance as consultants? What are some of the contradictions?

We often encounter consultants from the dominant social, racial, ethnic, gender, and cultural groups of society. Less frequently we see consultants who are minority group members. While these background characteristics play a role in any consultant's approach to the work, more significant to social change movements is the degree to which consulting educators approach their work from a critical perspective and an orientation towards transformation.

Certainly, the fact of having experienced poverty, sexism, racism, and/or discrimination does not necessarily mean that educators identify the social structure as the oppressive force. All of us, whether we're from minority or majority groups, are products of educational systems that trained us in the values of the dominant culture and its orientation to education. We are likely to

156

have internalized these values and approaches so we'll "fit in" better. We too struggle against our own resistance to alternative arrangements of social power.

In our work as consultants, then, we are conscious of our commitment to education not for the sake of disseminating information but for social change. But can an educator who has not and will never share the experience of the participants be able to work effectively to address their needs? For instance, under what conditions should male educators work to address issues such as male dominance and sexism? Or White educators work on the issue of racism? Can non-union educators understand unionists' issues?

In thinking through these questions, it is important to bear a few points in mind:

✦ Social change educators, no matter what their backgrounds, have to be clear on their stake in the issue under discussion. So a male can participate in a session on gender oppression as long as he recognizes that men are often the oppressors.

✦ Neither the money nor the fame are motivating factors for social change educators. Rather, their motivations come from the goal of empowering others to think critically and challenge unjust structures. We recognize, though, that these motivations are not always so clear cut and altruistic; there are diverse and even contradictory motivations in any one person.

✦ It is important to recognize the participants' social identities. For instance, if people of colour are not involved as educators in design and facilitation on anti-racist work, that work only reproduces dominant structures.

There are also benefits to having educators who share the same identity and experiences as the learners. This can make one less barrier to negotiate and one less aspect to explain: learners will usually assume that such educators share similar values, attitudes, and aspirations.

In essence, educators have to recognize the political side of their involvement in social change education. Either we understand our privilege and continue to exploit it; or we understand our privilege and create working conditions that both remove the blinkers of privilege and refuse to collapse into privilege.

For example, White educators should avoid anti-racist work where they are paid and people of colour are brought in as free "community labour". Men who believe in gender equity should continually protest participating in panels where only White men speak as experts. Social change educators with privileged social identities can either reinforce the "rightness" and "naturalness" of their privilege, or they can name it, challenge it, and refuse to collude in it whenever possible.

POWER
RELATIONS

Those of us committed to educating for social change attempt to be conscious always of the role and significance of power: who has it and who is powerless. Being aware of power is critical to an understanding of how it can be used to serve our needs and interests.

Power and social change educators

Our power as individual educators comes from any one or several of the following:

✦ **Information power** – where the educator possesses or has access to information that is perceived as valuable to others

✦ **Connection power** – based on the educator's "connections" with "influential or important" persons inside or outside of an organization

✦ **Expert power** – when the educator gains respect or has influence because she or he is perceived to possess expertise, skill, and knowledge

✦ **Position power** – when the educator's position as leader gives her or him the capacity to influence and obtain respect from others

✦ **Personality power** – where the educator is liked and admired by others because of his or her personality, and which means that participants sometimes identify with the educator

✦ **Network power** – where the educator is a member of, knows members of, or has established a network, which means that the educator is able to influence people.

This list indicates that educators usually enter a situation with a given form of power, and that the source of this power depends on the educators themselves, as well as on forces external to them.

The question is, given our goals as social change educators, how should we exercise this power, when, for what purpose, and under what conditions?

As social change educators we know that education should assist people in their personal development so they can achieve change in their lives and in society as a whole. Therefore we cannot afford to be ambivalent about our exercise of power. We must name the power, identify the source, and use it in a way that serves the interests and needs of the group we are working with.

Whatever the situation or setting – workshops, classroom, community – educators must establish a model for participants, particularly those engaged in social change and advocacy, of how to share ownership and responsibility. Power need not be seen as only a negative force. If we do look at it that way it will perpetuate ambivalence, which can become a stumbling block towards achieving social change.

Power and social identities

Social identity is another source of power. When we examine the social and cultural identities that characterize the dominant group, we get a sense of where power lies within the Canadian social structure.

We cannot ignore the extent to which power is socially constructed. By this we mean that regardless of our personal or political choices, our membership in particular social groups either endows us with or denies us privilege.

For example, even when an able-bodied woman is actively involved in the struggles of differently abled people for access to jobs, she still has a far better chance of getting a job than the people whose struggle she identifies with. Her opportunity is not a matter of her personal choice – it comes to her through the values of the dominant society. A person's power and influence vary with the number and types of dominant social and cultural characteristics possessed.

These social and cultural identities play a significant role in what people believe about who can wield influence. For example, a group of Black youth wanted to make a request of the executive director of their community centre. Their staff team was composed of a Black and a White worker. When the youth discussed who ought to talk with the director (who was White), they suggested that the White worker should do so. When asked why, they responded, "Because she is White."

In a "Train the Trainer" program for union educators, one of the facilitators, a woman, suggested that a man in the training team give individual feedback to two male union participants. Her suggestion was premised on the observation that the two participants in question heard critical comments more openly from the male facilitator than from the female.

The extent to which educators possess the social identities of the dominant group in Canada determines how their information is received. One Black facilitator recalls that in a multicultural training session, participants perceived him more as "a plant, a spy, an instigator, a shit-disturber, and a person who was bringing up racism unnecessarily" than as a facilitator equal to his White colleagues.

In another case, a Black educator was showing the film *Eye of the Storm* to a psychology class made up mostly of White students, on a day when the subject

was "Attitude" – with one of those attitudes being prejudice. The film is about a teacher teaching about prejudice to White primary grade students who live in an exclusively White community. A class member asked the educator if "he was trying to tell them something". Another asked, "Are you saying we're racist?" Although he was showing the film in the context of the course outline, his students interpreted the film as carrying a personal message from the educator. As in many situations, the participants linked the race of the facilitator to how they interpreted what they heard and to how much they accepted it.

Women and people of non-dominant racial and ethnic groups are faced with challenges that they must address if they are to work effectively with people from the dominant culture. Educators from the dominant group are less likely to meet resistance and can use their privilege consciously, responsibly, and strategically to assist educators who are limited by their social position. There's an example of this in chapter four, "MAKING THE MOST OF WHO WE ARE." In that case, as a White person, the facilitator knew that her racial identity did not distract the White participants from their own task of examining racism.

The benefits of recognizing the role of social identities

A White educator who conducts courses in cross-culturalism says she does not tell "students" (young people) about her ethnic background because "it is not relevant" and she doesn't want to influence the students' interaction with her. Nevertheless, she expects the students to talk about their own backgrounds.

In another situation, a White facilitator doing an anti-racist workshop began by asking the only two non-Whites of the fourteen participants to tell the rest of the group about their experiences with racism. One Black participant objected, suggesting it was unfair to use the two of them as data and not invite everyone, including the Whites, to share their experiences with racism, particularly because of their dominant social position.

As social change educators we always need to acknowledge our social identities and the role they play in learning situations. Educators and all other participants, whatever the context, should share knowledge, ideas, and experiences equally. Doing so takes the mystery out of the role and helps to see that power is shared. Moreover, the process enhances communication and comfort.

Educators who are women and people of colour are very aware that they cannot remain the "objective facilitator" in workshops. Participants certainly don't see them that way.

Consider, for example, a Black woman facilitating a workshop on race relations and cross-culturalism, when the majority of the participants are White. She never talks of her nationality, race, ethnicity, or culture. Nevertheless the participants, based on what they see as her background characteristics, treat her according to their expectations. But if the workshop has a White female facilitator, the participants assume she is a Canadian; no further information is necessary.

As social change educators, we must be conscious about the role that skin colour, gender, sexual orientation, and accent play in the learning situation. We need to consciously evaluate our feelings and share our ideas like all other participants.

RICK ARNOLD

Sharing power   For the social change educator, sharing power, real or perceived, is necessary if we are to make the process of learning democratic and engage all participants in analysis and setting goals and directions.

When we recognize the role of social identities, we make it possible to hear what participants are saying and understand what they mean. We are able to avoid being defensive when "accused" of being "White", "Male", or "English". We place ourselves in the same vulnerable position as the participants, which makes it possible to build trust and effective communication.

Whatever the setting – workshop, classroom, community – early on educators must acknowledge their own power base as well as that of all the participants, particularly the power of social identity and the power accorded by the position of "educator" (even one who constructs participatory activities). To achieve full participation everyone must feel equal, important, and committed to the process.

We have to remember, too, that even when we take up the many concrete methods of acknowledging and sharing power (as outlined in chapter four) or engage in the many possible activities (chapter three), educators still have power because of their role in shaping the process; or because of most people's presumption that educators know more.

161

The educator as facilitator and learner

Traditionally, the educational process has placed learners in a passive position. In Paulo Freire's words, they have been looked on as "empty vessels". For social change educators, however, learners are people who have something to teach. Such a stance goes a long way towards overcoming differences in the background and life experiences of educators and learners.

The educator is a facilitator and a resource person, someone who engages people in a dialogue that is a two-way conversation. The learners in the educational process are active participants, individuals who respond and help shape that process.

For a new educator/learner relationship to take hold, the educational setting has to be supportive – which means that people do not get jumped on for expressing their ideas. After all, we are trying to build people who are aware and wish to advocate and work for change collectively.

When learners are able to participate actively in the process, what happens is as much of their own making as it is of the facilitator's making. They share responsibility for the results. Learners should be challenged to help shape their situation, which also means becoming critically aware of it. Facilitators should be open to challenges from participants.

The ability to listen and learn from participants builds mutual respect. It affirms the dignity of all; it is the basis of empowerment. To listen is to be on an equal footing; listening means putting yourself in the place of the other. How can educators construct a setting in which there isn't a growing "we versus them", no matter how genuine our intent to do otherwise? Especially for educators in formal school settings, the art of listening is an important pillar in building structures that counteract some deeply ingrained, top-down teaching habits.

At the base of all this is the educator's genuine belief in people's potential and willingness to let go of some power and control. An authentic relationship of dialogue cannot be built by following guidelines or principles; people will "feel" the underlying belief and trust of the educator. Becoming honest, open, and vulnerable is not easy; it is a struggle.

RICK ARNOLD

INCREASING
OUR IMPACT

In our experience, elements that allow our work to have a greater impact include working collectively, being able to size up or assess a situation we face, keeping an eye open for opportunities, and acknowledging the contradictions and being clear about our limitations in tackling the dominant agenda.

Assess the situation

Before starting a workshop session, for instance, we clarify the expectations (with a planning team ahead of time if possible). We find out about issues in the organization as well as in the wider social context so we can understand and address them.

In the workshop itself we find out about expectations from participants and check to see how those expectations relate to the objectives of the planning team or those who hired us. Whatever the situation, we make clear our role and help structure sessions that will allow for critical reflection by participants and include next steps or an action component.

Grab the free space

We constantly need to be looking for cracks in the dominant agenda, where the powerful and influential disagree among themselves. In the late 1980s-early 1990s, for instance, industry and government consensus has been faltering around issues such as the environment or free trade. This faltering allows popular organization to take the lead and suggest alternatives.

Timing is all important for an action to be successful. We should ensure that people are ready at any given moment to participate in initiatives addressing their concerns and issues. What kind of "free space" is available to introduce particular kinds of social change activities?

In our experience, each new situation kicks up opportunities for action and suggests when it is best to take action. The important thing is to recognize that the opportunity exists and get a foot in before the door slams shut again.

Acknowledge the contradictions in the work

Educators from outside an organization face different dynamics and contradictions than their counterparts inside. Getting the rank and file to look critically at society (if that is an objective, for instance) can also entail putting the organization under a magnifying glass to see if it is part of the solution or part of the problem. This approach can feel threatening to an executive if a reappraisal of the organization's stance and hiring practices was not what the executive bargained for in hiring an outsider to do a specific piece of work with the membership. At the same time, outsiders must recognize their different stakes and appreciate the risks for insiders.

If the workers speak out, they could be subject to retribution from an insecure executive. Educators also run the risk of never being invited back again when an executive and/or a chastened rank and file come to see them as "shit-disturbers". That is one of the reasons why, when we work with another organization as "outsiders", the objectives for the session/work need to be clear; and why we attempt when possible to involve both participants and the inviter/organizer/executive members to help form part of a planning and design

163

group to set guidelines for what is possible and identify what might constitute "stepping over the line".

Sometimes we end up feeling more allied with people in subordinate positions than with the leadership that has brought us in. It is a delicate tightrope act and many factors have to be considered, including, for example, the extent of the relationship, length of contract, and potential for change within the organization.

For the "insider" who works full-time for an organization, there will be some contradictions between what the organization says and what it does. Again, many feathers can easily get ruffled at all levels – and sometimes it may be necessary to ruffle them if there is to be a positive breakthrough. Inside educators need patience and skill to reaffirm the positive and improve upon the shortcomings.

Particularly in organizations that are membership-based, social change educators will want to see the voice from below strengthened. Part of this process will involve increasing the feeling of ownership that the rank and file members feel towards their organization.

Work collectively   There is a tremendous benefit in working collectively with educators from different backgrounds. We have found it invaluable to have at least two people facilitating and planning a session instead of the traditional one person. As social change educators, we must model anti-racism, employment equity, and awareness of international issues in our practice by having the team of educators reflect the diversity in our society.

Even if the learner population is a homogeneous White population, we still need to reflect that diversity. Whether such a homogeneous population is dealing explicitly with racial concerns or other issues (such as how to facilitate board meetings), we should make every effort to involve non-dominant group educators to reflect Canada's current population mix.

This practice also challenges stereotypes, exposes non-dominant group members to the organizations we work with, and models different working relationships. The other side of this coin is the heavy price paid by non-dominant group educators in cases where they are working to educate the dominant group without any allies from that group.

BARB THOMAS

Help to give voice to others and promote their presence

As social change educators, we have a responsibility to challenge the perception of the educator as "expert" or "all-knowing". We have to demystify how knowledge is produced and bring everyone to the understanding that they have a role in the production of knowledge; and that they can gain access to "expert" knowledge of various sorts when they decide such access would indeed be useful.

A good example of this problem is the practice of research, a knowledge-producing vehicle. Often research is seen as a process in which an "objective expert" (usually an outsider) gathers information in an "objective manner". It has results (by way of recommendations) that are produced without the input or consent of the people it affects. Usually research done by an outsider comes back in the form of power forged with what has been taken (or stolen) from the people who participated in the research. Often it comes back to exploit.

There are other approaches to research. Participatory research, for instance, can be a vehicle for educating, facilitating collective analysis, and developing change strategies. Participatory research material can be a tool for advocacy and giving voice to the participants who otherwise would not have a chance to be heard. This approach involves being inclusive and promotes action for change. It recognizes an ideological basis for documentation and aims to demystify how information is gathered and knowledge is produced. It emphasizes the collective nature of analysis, seeing all participants as investigators.

Finally, writing for social change is oriented towards action; it is not research for "the sake of research". The researcher who uses participatory approaches sets the research agenda in co-operation with participants, based on their perceived needs and issues. Together, they reflect on and analyse the information. The emphasis is always on giving the participants presence in the process and in the information.

This approach is evident in those works that give insight into the experiences and perceptions of non-dominant groups, while at the same time placing their interpretations and perspectives on the agenda for those of us committed to helping them address their issues.* Such works take seriously the contributions of everyone towards creating knowledge, with the belief that the creation of knowledge is not just the prerogative of "experts". People are able to read other people's ideas and see that others share their concerns.

Readers of such materials will get the message that it is legitimate to express their concerns and that their views will be respected when expressed. On this basis, the expression of their issues and concerns helps to bring about social change.

* For examples of participatory research see such works as: Carl James, *Seeing Ourselves* and *Making It*; Michael Czerny, S.J. and Jamie Swift, *Getting Started on Social Analysis in Canada*; and Patricia Maguire, *Doing Participatory Research*.

A VITAL BRIDGE   We gain a sense of satisfaction when the needs and issues of the people we work with are being addressed; when it is clear that prior assumptions have been challenged and the next steps to bring about change have been outlined. Here are some of the comments that have communicated this kind of growth to us.

> *I've had some real Ah-Hahs – like "That's what I've been doing all along, but I never saw it that way before...".*

> *I gain confidence in being able to tackle work which lay ahead.*

> *From a sense of being alone and isolated in this work to a new appreciation of working with others who themselves are facing similar problems.*

> *I've gained confidence, self-esteem, new energy, new knowledge, and new friends.*

These responses illustrate shifts that nourish us in our work and give us energy for the work ahead. We are always conscious that the process of education for social change needs commitment and belief in the goal. That is why we build and seek feedback from participants.

Educators too, are encouraged, given energy, and get excited about new opportunities, new networks, and new friendships with people who share similar goals and ideals. Participant feedback is a vital bridge in the interdependence between educators and learners.

Because we are often swimming against the current as we challenge inequitable ideas and practices, we need to support each other – just as learners need support so they can gain confidence in their capacity to bring about change.

When everyone takes responsibility for the learning, everyone is a teacher. This brings with it a sense of freedom, of liberation from the traditional responsibility of a top-down educator. The greater social solidarity to which we aspire needs to be mirrored in a solidarity between ourselves and learners, as we continuously support each other's movement towards transformation.

MARK HENDERSON

166

6

Looking Ahead:

Implications for our Work in the 1990s

6 LOOKING FORWARD: Implications for our work in the 1990's

5 LOOKING BACK: Issues emerging from our practice

3 SHAPING OUR TOOLS: Developing and Using Activities

2 WORKING BY DESIGN: Putting together a program

4 WORKING ON OUR FEET: The practice of democratic facilitation

1 THIS IS OUR CHANCE: Educating Strategically

On the eve of the 21st century the experts are hard at work charting and predicting future shock. At the DMI we're wondering about what's in store for Canadian educators and activists too, and we've decided to try and put some of our thoughts on paper.

We have no "expert" pretensions of having the final say. Rather, we hope our musings might act as a catalyst for your discussion on future directions, as it has for ours. In the spirit of lateral thinking, we invite you to consider not so much what's "right" or "wrong" about these comments, but what's "interesting" in them.

In general we feel that some tough challenges lie ahead – but they are challenges that will provide opportunities for social change workers. There are probably too many of these challenges to fit within the covers of one book, let alone one chapter, so here we've settled on twelve discussion areas or sites of struggle. We've grouped them loosely into four categories, recognizing that each site has multiple layers that often spill over into other categories. We think these are all challenges that are critical to the success of a social change agenda.

But first, a word about agendas in general. We live in a political and socio-economic system that benefits some people more than others. We believe that this situation has not evolved "naturally" but by design. Those with wealth and power strive to maintain a position of privilege, and their decisions help shape the direction our society takes. Theirs is a dominant agenda: it operates from a position of power.

This agenda is constantly being reshaped as the world around it changes. It can also be subject to inter-elite rivalries as economic empires collide. Viewed from below, the dominant agenda is often seen as monolithic. But we would be short-sighted if we didn't look for the cracks in the wall.

In response there's a popular agenda, which can be well or poorly organized. Often defensive in an age of privatization and cutbacks, the popular agenda can and does develop its own vision of a future society that will benefit the majority. The popular agenda is sometimes deeply divided – kept fighting on one front or issue to the exclusion of everything else. Its quota of power starts from nil and increases slowly with the level of organization and determination.

So here, under each heading representing one of the twelve future challenges, we have subheadings of "dominant agenda" and "popular agenda". To the popular agenda we have added implications for educators. In our view there is no doubt we will be identifying with the popular agenda rather than trying to build something separate.

Part of the role we can play as educators is to uncover the often hidden components of the dominant agenda and help strengthen the organizing efforts of the popular sector. Though supportive, we can't be uncritical of any popular agenda that simply exchanges one oppressive structure for another. This is the essence of our concern about democratic practice being built into organizations while they are still in opposition. The way we work today will be an indication of the society we will build tomorrow.

ECONOMIC
CHALLENGES

**Canada's economic
future at stake**

The dominant agenda

In the 1980s they called it privatization, deficit reduction, structural adjust-ment, and a host of other technical-sounding names. What they meant was muzzle government regulators, reduce corporate taxes, cut back on "costly" social programs, and, most importantly, give business a freer hand in an expanded market, in other words, Free Trade.

In the 1960s and 1970s, social upheavals led some people to question the role that corporations played in society. So the 1980s became a time for large companies to fix up their image and rebuild public trust in their "stewardship". Reagan and Thatcher became the standard-bearers for the corporate line that in the world's current sorry state the governments and not the private sector are to blame.

Canada's Progressive Conservative Party rode the crest of this logic to two electoral victories in the 1980s. Increasingly, investors and financiers could do no wrong. Questionable practices such as corporate cannibalism, leveraged buyouts, insider trading, and real estate flips – to name just a few – provoked rel-atively little public reaction (partly because these practices were clouded in mys-tifying language and often dismissed as purely commercial concerns with no political or social implications). *

But in helping "shift the blame" towards government and away from the pri-vate sector, Canada's mainstream politicians painted themselves into a corner. Any mention of increased public spending or new taxes is now bound to get a lot of adverse public reaction.

Through it all the corporate image-makers have been highly successful at damage control and blame shifting. And we should expect more of the same in the 1990s.

DEBORAH BARNDT

* By corporate cannibalism we mean the practice of some companies whose purpose in buying out other companies is to dismember them and sell off their parts for a profit. A leveraged buyout is the corporate practice of borrowing large sums of money (often from banks) against the assets of the company being bid on.

The popular agenda/implications for educators

We can see the results of the dominant agenda on our streets today. The number of food banks continues to grow. Longer lineups at more food banks accompany an upsurge in BMW sales. Wealthy Canadians talk about expanding free trade to the Americas while working-class people experience plant and office shutdowns that push jobs south of the border and thousands of employees out on the pavement. What is good for a few has not turned out to be fair treatment for the many.

Anti-poverty organizations, unions, churches, environmental groups, students, and communities are among those fighting the painful measures. Many are affiliated at the national level to the Pro-Canada Network. Coalition strategies like PCN have been tried before with mixed results. One problem in the past was that vanguard politics often brought along the hidden agendas of an elite leadership and/or an attempt to submerge difference in the rank and file.

In the 1990s educators for social change can support a new style of coalition, one that allows a broad, representative voice to emerge to challenge current economic policies. Critical to moving our collective economic agenda onto the front burner will be the new solidarity emerging between community groups and unions. It's a meeting of quality of life issues and the core of economic resistance. As educators for social change we need to be active in these coalitions. Our specific skills can help build trust based on what we have in common and respect for our differences.

Coalition-building is not easy, because groups may share some common interests and be in opposing camps on others. And there is the very real question of power struggles within sectors and organizations and with people who try to control agendas.

An area that needs more attention is "organizational culture". At the DMI we feel work in this area is critical to future joint efforts to help one group understand not only how another works but also what the possibilities and limitations are. Social change educators can also help coalition members shape processes that can lead to the development of an alternative economic project.

Lifting the last frontiers: capital and resistance go global

The dominant agenda

Over the past twenty-five years many transnational corporations became private empires with sales greater than the Gross National Products of some Third World nations. Although these companies have spread their investments to most corners of the globe, they are still facing many irritants in their world-wide capital accumulation plans. Some Third World countries, for example, continue to insist that a share of the profits of foreign corporations made on their soil be reinvested locally.

In the 1990s, conditions are changing, giving investors new confidence. The Soviet empire is disintegrating, and the big three economic powers – Japan, Europe, and the United States – now predominate. Eastern Europe is open for business and Third World countries are no longer able to play the United States off against the Soviet Union. Three megatrading blocs seem to be emerging, each one built around a major economic power with all other participants becoming the junior partners. Debt is the lever used to persuade reluctant nations to participate in this new international economic order.

Policing these arrangements continues to be the job of the International Monetary Fund (IMF) and the World Bank. The advice these institutions give to poorer nations (backed up by a threat of no more loans or investment dollars) sounds familiar to most Canadians by now: "Cut government spending; cut social programs (where they exist); bring down trade barriers; and give private investors a free hand." This advice creates a red carpet for transnational corporations preparing to play countries off against each other while seeking unrestricted access to their cheap labour and raw materials.

DEBORAH BARNDT

171

The popular agenda/implications for educators

Spiralling Third World debt became a major issue for the popular agenda in the 1980s. Today citizens of Third World nations know through bitter experience that the IMF's structural adjustments mean greater sacrifice for an already impoverished majority. They are taking to the streets to fight price rises, cutbacks, and layoffs as their governments cave in to restructuring pressures.

They're humming the same tune in Ottawa these days, which makes a "foreign" problem sound familiar, providing us with a logical starting point for work around international economic issues. Some non-governmental organizations – for example, OXFAM, CUSO and the Toronto Committee for the Liberation of Southern Africa (TCLSAC) – are developing popular education sessions that link the structural adjustment programs we see in Third World countries with the Conservative agenda in Canada, making these vague international concepts more real and concrete in the examples of our daily lives.

In our hemisphere the Free Trade agenda is a testing ground for international solidarity. Canadian jobs are being lost as corporations shift production to non-union plants in the United States or to the even cheaper labour area on the Mexico-U.S. border known as the maquiladoras. A real danger exists that the victims in each country will blame each other rather than the real culprits.

With this in mind, a project called Common Frontiers has been formed to tackle this cross-boundary corporate initiative. A brainchild of the Latin American Working Group in Toronto, Common Frontiers has grown to involve many affiliates of the Canadian Labour Congress (CLC). The Pro-Canada Network has endorsed it and the Ecumenical Coalition for Economic Justice (ECEJ) has done some excellent research for it.

Popular educators need to support initiatives such as Common Frontiers that bring Canadians into direct contact with counterparts in other countries. We can play a part in helping build a strong sense of equal partnership that crosses language and cultural differences. If we can help foster an openness to learn from other experiences and value opinions coming from outside Canada's borders, we are on our way to making common cause in tackling capital's global agenda.

But the mere existence of strong international opposition to the global corporate agenda is not enough. Through exchanges, workshops, and conferences, we need to support the building of workable alternatives to present economic trends in Canada. In the process we need to draw on the wealth of experience that our southern partners have. They too are likely to be interested in any insights we have to offer on a common goal of restructuring the world economic order from the bottom up. Who said it was the "trickle-up" effect?

172

**The "human
resources"
talk back**

The dominant agenda

There is much discussion in corporate and government circles of "human resources". People are seen as factors of production, to be moved geographically and slotted functionally according to the needs of the planners. In this discourse, "critical shortages" are announced, and "building a competitive workforce" becomes a top priority.

On the receiving end of this agenda are the increasing numbers of Canadians caught at the "bad jobs" end of an increasingly polarized labour market. People are on the move, from Schefferville to Montreal, from Kimberley to Vancouver. Their paths are shaped by economic decisions over which they have no control, and the impacts on family and community life are their own problem.

Completely absent from most human resources thinking are the people who are unemployed, underemployed, or in a low-wage service sector job. For them, not being considered part of the workforce shuts the door on opportunity.

The human resources perspective is damaging enough domestically, but its blind spots are highlighted in the treatment of immigrants. The majority of Canada's immigrants now come from the Third World and are expected to take jobs at low wage rates. However, immigrants who enter with money get preference. Meanwhile the policy debate on immigration focuses on expanding the consumer market and increasing the population to counteract emigration and the low domestic birthrate. Competition among workers, regionally and internationally, is the name of the game.

DMI ARCHIVES

173

The popular agenda/implications for educators

Working people are more than factors of production. They require security, dignity, and creativity in their jobs, and this is a power issue. Individual workers cannot exercise power, but the collective decision to give or withhold intelligent co-operation has major economic implications. This decision is exercised through trade unions.

During the last generation, unions in the United States have lost ground: they've gone from representing 30 per cent of the workforce to less than 20 per cent. In the same period unions in Canada have gained strength, moving from representing 30 per cent to nearly 40 per cent. Working with this increasingly confident and outward-looking social institution is quite different for an activist educator in Canada than it is for our colleagues in the United States. Nonetheless, as the Conservative/corporate agenda in Canada gets implanted through privatization, deregulation, and free trade, the very existence of unions is being threatened.

Unions are not immune from the prejudices, sexism, and racism that affect all other Canadian institutions. Individual members tend to see immigrants as taking away jobs or as being a drain on our economy and welfare system. This is blaming the victim. Similarly, many unionists fear that current members will be undercut by immigrants, who come motivated to struggle hard to make a better life for themselves and their children. Educators within the trade union movement, in co-operation with some outsiders, are developing courses and materials on employment equity to address such fears and challenge the racism that allows the economic establishment to divide and conquer.

A major challenge for educators is to develop our own capacity to bridge cultural divisions and to commit ourselves to a practice of mutual respect and inclusion. This commitment may also mean joining in struggles led by cultural groups demanding equal rights, employment equity, changes to immigration policy, and full participation in economic decision-making.

POLITICAL
CHALLENGES

**First Nations on the
move**

The dominant agenda

For the First Nations of the Americas, through the last five hundred years of conquest and settlement the dominant imposed agenda has been the White agenda. Whether facing the results of Europeans shipping "new world" gold back to Queen Isabella or fencing in a homestead on land with no apparent owner, the aboriginal peoples have been robbed and bloodied by superior firepower. The perception of Indians as "savages" has endured, reproduced over and over in cowboy movies rerunning on TV or available at the video store.

The conquest of the First Nations did not come easy and over the years there have been major rebellions against White rule. Eventual pacification often included the signing of a peace treaty in which the Whites graciously ceded some marginal lands to Native habitation. Today a paternalistic network of government payments and services has been structured around Native reserves. Many government officials and industry executives still view the aboriginal peoples and their way of life as an obstacle to progress. Even some immigrants who suffer daily discrimination themselves have come to see Indians from the dominant perspective.

Lands once thought useless and ceded to the First Nations now sit on oil reserves or precious minerals, and the pressure is on to move Native people off those lands. Successive Canadian governments have been content to just keep talking about past treaty promises rather than honouring them. But the events of summer 1990 at Kanesatake/Oka in Quebec proved that state force will be used if Native people do not behave "with moderation" in pursuing future demands.

DEBORAH BARNDT

The popular agenda/implications for educators

There is a new element of militancy backing up the demands of Canada's First Nations for fair treatment in the 1990s. The confrontation at Kanesatake/Oka struck a chord with the people of the First Nations across Canada, as witnessed by the many solidarity road blocks that went up around the country. The time for talking for its own sake is over and the moment for meaningful negotiation has arrived. The scuttling of Meech Lake in Manitoba by Elijah Harper, a Native member of the provincial legislature, was a firm reminder that Canada's indigenous people need to be treated as nations – no more second-class citizenship. Sovereignty and self-government have been put firmly on the public agenda and will have to be dealt with, or further militancy can be expected.

Against all odds, First Nations have been able to maintain their cultural traditions. Native artists have developed a strong arts-community link in many large urban centres across the country. Cultural communication has been a vehicle for the expression of aboriginal concerns and has provided a foot in the door of mainstream media. Greater media exposure to First Nations' values and outlook has begun to have a profound effect on how other Canadians view the world around them. Education continues to be a site of struggle for Native communities, which are rejecting the residential school system that separates off their young people. Community members are grappling with the questions of accountability and control over education on their own lands.

Aboriginal educators, their communities, and diverse cultures may also challenge some of the basic assumptions non-Natives have about how education happens. The consensus model of decision-making or the "medicine wheel" concept of learning engenders non-linear and perhaps ultimately more deeply democratic practices. Aboriginal educators also bring new perspectives on the role of culture and spirituality in our work.

Non-Native popular educators are being challenged to take seriously the voice of First Nations participants in workshops. But we should be thinking not only about the odd chance for them to speak, but also about having Native people as part of our planning, design, and facilitation teams. At conferences we help to plan, we need to ensure that the organizers whose organizations are usually on record as opposing Canada's treatment of First Nations include the Native agenda in their programs.

To develop longer-term alliances with First Nations people, the question of trust will be central. Such trust will have to be earned through clear support for Native sovereignty and from the development of equal partnerships where mutual learning can occur.

DEBORAH BARNDT

176

Sovereignty and association

The dominant agenda

The 1990s have ushered in a global trend to greater cultural self-determination. The space for the accommodation of cultural difference is still to be gauged, but globally the issue could lead to the breakup of many larger countries.

In Canada, demands from Quebec as well as from the First Nations challenge the traditional concept of one nation running sea to sea. It used to be that capital both in Quebec and the rest of Canada would fight talk of separation. Now capital in Quebec is not so concerned about separating as long as there is no fundamental systemic shakeup along the way. With the advent of Free Trade, the trade and investment axis is shifting significantly to north-south and away from east-west. The rest of corporate Canada can accommodate separation more easily now than in 1980.

Quebec entrepreneurs increasingly want to get out from under the anglo shadow, and here their interests combine with other sectors of Quebec society. For many of those other sectors, the cultural questions loom largest when in fact their deeper economic interests may be quite at odds.

RYAN REMIORZ - CANAPRESS

177

The popular agenda/implications for educators

A majority of Québécois are fed up with their treatment by the rest of Canada and are ready for a change. The trade unions, community, and other grassroots organizations see ending anglo domination as an opportunity to build something new and different. They bring a radical edge to change in Quebec's future status in relation to Canada.

Those of us working for social change in English-speaking Canada need to support a rethinking of the concept of nationhood. In the process we may very well run up against reactionary elements. We should try not to silence them but begin to deal with their comments as we move towards a new Canadian construct. The ability of organizers, activists, and educators to help shape a social change agenda is closely related to the degree of openness established in dealing with difference. Increasingly, part of our work will be confronting the fears that we all have about "the other", looking at where those fears come from as well as exploring the positive contributions that people of different cultures and backgrounds are making in our society. In the process we will also need to confront some very real conflicts of interests based on those differences.

Many of us living in English Canada have been cut off from the important developments of popular education and popular resistance in Quebec, sometimes because we are simply oblivious to events there. We need to work hard to break down those barriers, enter into an exchange with our Quebec counterparts, and learn from their rich experience.

Educators in the rest of Canada, whether or not they agree with Quebec sovereignty, must respect Quebec's right to self-determination. Regardless of the outcome, it will be important to build a strong association between popular sector work happening in both contexts.

Separateness does not diminish the importance of continuing to struggle around the issues of language and culture that have often divided us and limited communication. Rather, it increases the importance of a horizontal approach between equals, respectful of difference. This approach may succeed where vertically imposed solutions like Meech Lake or ideological assumptions that don't take cultural differences into account have failed. Success is important if we are to first maintain and then strengthen popular sector unity, all the while collectively navigating through the difficult waters.

SOCIAL
CHALLENGES

**Deeds not words:
feminizing our
practice**

The dominant agenda

Governments and corporations have recognized the problem of women's job ghettos and unfair pay practices, but the problems remain. Although a few booted and suited women have made it into the boys club, male privilege in the workplace and society in general is still the norm. Women who have spoken out about sexuality, reproduction, and family life have faced a patriarchal backlash, which among other things challenges their right to control their own bodies.

As a society we have only just begun to recognize the level of violence against women in the home and to see that it is part of a deeply ingrained pattern of male behaviour where being "in charge" is what is "to be expected". There is still tremendous pressure, in the media and in some Canadian religious institutions for example, to deny that incidents of violence such as the Montreal massacre of fourteen women in December 1989 are anything more than random acts.

The popular agenda/implications for educators

Most politicians and company executives agree with the concept of having more women in decision-making positions, but the old-boy network is very much alive and selects its own members.

Women in the 1990s will continue to fight for better legislation on employment and pay equity in the workplace. A growing number of popular organizations have women's caucuses as an integral part of their decision-making structures. There is also a trend among established women's organizations to incorporate questions of race and class in their equity demands, opening the door to closer working ties not only with the labour movement but also with differently abled and working-class women and women of colour.

Social change education, even when its focus is not on gender, needs to learn from feminist theory, especially where it links the personal and the political. At the DMI we feel that middle-class White feminists in the women's movement need to work closely and equally with women of colour and working-class women. We also believe that we must all model different ways of working that challenge the type of exclusive networks based on privilege that we abhor in the old-boys network.

Popular organizations and unions still dominated by men will be challenged by women impatient with organizations that fight for social change but still mirror gender inequities themselves. In designing and facilitating education sessions, popular educators need to ensure a voice for the broad range of women of different abilities, background, age, colour, and sexual preference. These voices need to be built into our teams, our print and audio-visuals, our issues, and our work processes.

Confronting White privilege

The dominant agenda

Canada has a long and unsavoury history of racism. The White Europeans who settled Canada pushed the original inhabitants aside to stake their claim. The Whites imported some Blacks as slaves and by law actively discouraged other Blacks from moving here. Those Blacks who did manage to immigrate over the past 150 years, particularly to Nova Scotia and Ontario, were accorded second-class citizenship and denied basic rights.

Earlier this century prospective Chinese immigrants had to pay a special head tax before being allowed into Canada. The story is much the same for people from places or with backgrounds not considered desirable by Canadian officials.

An expanding industry and agriculture required more immigrants to do manual work. Initial recruitment efforts were aimed at mainly attracting poor Whites from Europe, but gradually this pattern changed.

Today Canada chooses 75 per cent of its immigrants from Third World countries. Now about one in three residents in Metro Toronto was born in another country and most communities of colour are growing faster than White communities. While racism is increasingly recognized as a Canadian problem, the system and ideas that perpetuate racism are still intact – in the workplace, in our institutions, and in our communities.

The current official term for promoting harmony is "multiculturalism". This concept, promulgated by the federal government since 1971, avoids the more sinister aspects of the "melting pot" theory once prevalent in the United States but obscures the historical and newer roots of Canadian racism. Recent police shootings of Blacks in Toronto and Montreal, unrest in Nova Scotia, and the events at Kanesatake/Oka are just a few of the indicators of a deep and pervasive racism avoided by the multiculturalists.

The dominant agenda of multiculturalism, when pursued, focuses on remedying individual cases of unacceptable behaviour while avoiding the systemic practices that exert the real impact. When impatience and anger at persistent injustice mobilize communities, as in Toronto or at Oka, the dominant forces attempt to separate the moderates from the militants and to name their preferred community leaders, dividing communities and trying to dilute their strength to fight back.

The popular agenda/implications for educators

Black activists are challenging racist structures and attitudes embedded in White-dominated police forces. School trustees of colour along with progressive White counterparts are pushing for curriculum that challenges racist stereotypes and practices. Unfair hiring practices persist.

But there is strong pressure on legislators to bring in laws like the Employment Equity Act with goals and timetables for visible minorities, as well as for women, Native people, and the differently abled. Artists and cultural workers of colour are demanding that both dominant and oppositional cultural organizations examine their policies for hiring, decision-making, programming, and allocation of resources.

Anti-racist education is an area that popular educators – White, people of colour, and Native people – need to be directing more energy to in the 1990s. However, to do so we have to be clear about our different stakes in this work. Those of us who are White traditionally have not had to deal critically with our cultural identity – it is "the norm". For Black educators, cultural identity is an ever present factor and always an issue. Increasingly, all of us as educators need to deal as honestly and openly as possible with who we are, so we can help others in our workshops do the same.

Anti-racist education also requires rethinking about who plans and facilitates the sessions. Our preference is that wherever possible in a team of two, at least one will be a person of colour. To practise what we preach, we need to ensure that popular organizations involve people of colour as full partners, being mindful of the problem of taking people away from their bases where they are often most needed. It is also crucial that the materials we produce carry the voices of people of colour and Native people in the text as well as in the visuals – and without falling into tokenism.

In addition, an anti-racist approach to social change education involves exposing the limits of multiculturalism, challenging White activists to see the racism so apparent to its targets, joining with activists of colour in their struggles for equity, and resisting all efforts to keep "the militants" shut off on the margins.

Taking back the Grey Agenda

The dominant agenda

Older people today fare little better than the many disposable items our industries produce. Advertising in a consumer society such as Canada's places a premium on youth culture, constantly reminding us all – no matter what our age – that young is beautiful. Management, influenced just as much by its own advertising as you or I, places a premium on adaptability and mobility in an era of rapid technological change. The doors just seem to close the older you get.

Most people, once they are counted out of the labour pool, fall back into paternalistic state hands that seek to "serve them", "amuse them", or "use them" to continue the pattern – rather than incorporate their experience or knowledge into self-managed endeavours. In recent years the government has treated the Canada Pension Plan not so much as a right for every citizen in recognition for contributions to the workforce but as a luxury, a prime territory for cutbacks.

Inequities that hit women, racial minorities, and other non-dominant groups before retirement age are compounded afterwards. The result for many is a time of grinding poverty and continued second-class status.

DEBORAH BARNDT

The popular agenda/implications for educators

Not all older people accept being put on the shelf. Some are speaking out at public forums, through the media, or in books to challenge dominant perspectives on ageing. Others, like British Columbia's Raging Grannies, provide an alternative perspective on a variety of issues, using cultural forms such as drama and song.

In the process they challenge societal stereotypes about older minds and abilities. In the mid-1980s older people were the first group to organize and successfully oppose the Conservative government's attempt to cut back pensions as part of its structural adjustment program.

In the 1990s it is evident that many older people are becoming aware of the needs in their own communities and of their responsibility to use their knowledge to help find solutions. Such needs include lack of housing, overuse of prescription drugs, and ethical decisions regarding use of modern technology – as well as the need to work for peace and a liveable environment.

As social change educators we have to be aware that in the everyday life of many communities, older people are at work using their experience and concern, helping one another in building a more humane world.

In workshops with both older and younger participants, it will be increasingly important to discuss ageism and how it can divide us in the same way that racism and sexism do. Younger educators need to work at developing relationships with older people, since so much in our society segregates us by age. Seniors represent a tremendous pool of volunteer energy and knowledge and can bring leadership and labour to many of the struggles we work on.

All of us have a stake in combating ageism. Where possible we should draw from examples of the very different treatment given older people in aboriginal cultures and in other societies beyond our borders. This understanding can help us guard against unconsciously reproducing dominant paternalistic attitudes in our work.

Seniors and their organizations may need support from social change educators. At the DMI we are currently working with activist Doris Marshall to plan and implement leadership training sessions for older people so that they can become the subjects of – rather than the objects of – later life programming.

183

A matter of
planetary survival

The dominant agenda

Environmental destruction has emerged as one of the hot issues of the 1990s –
after long decades when politicians and industry largely dismissed earlier warn-
ings as the "price of progress".

For the last two centuries, capitalism operated on the understanding that
the world was an infinite storehouse of resources that were "ours" to exploit.
Now, faced with clear evidence that there are limits to what the earth can bear,
some executives are having to re-evaluate the basic premise of "expand or die".

Resource extractive industries still view more stringent government guidelines as irritants that will hurt profits. Manufacturers, usually located in more
populated areas, often come under close community scrutiny, particularly for
obvious breaches of air pollution standards or dumping practices. But both the
resource and manufacturing sectors still seem to be dragging their heels on
cleanups or installation of new, clean technology.

There is some movement at the retail business level as supermarkets and
other outlets see possible profits and good public relations in marketing environmentally friendly "green" products. But other companies are just becoming more
sophisticated at appearing to be ecologically sound, with their glossy ads of rain
forests intended to mark their contribution to the exploitation of labour and land
at home and abroad.

Although public opinion in Canada supports the idea of government getting
tough on corporations that misrepresent their products or pollute, the companies warn that they can and will close down and move to areas where legislation
to protect the environment is non-existent.

The popular agenda/implications for educators

The people and organizations who have long worked to save the environment
and have been ridiculed for it now see their work paying off. Public awareness
has been helped in no small way by real events: nuclear disasters, oil spills,
barges full of garbage that nobody wants, beaches off limits to bathers, and the
fear of global warming, to name a few. Although we are becoming more aware of
the fragility of the natural world around us, we nevertheless remain to a greater
or lesser degree participants in a consumer lifestyle often tied into ecological
destruction.

Environmental activists have shown an exemplary balance of policy lobbying with grassroots mobilization. In Canada and other northern countries, environmental groups are putting forward concrete plans to tackle the crisis. In the
midst of the 1990 Ontario elections, for example, Greenpeace, Pollution Probe,
Citizens for a Safe Environment, and the Nuclear Awareness Project joined to
present politicians with a practical blueprint for future regulatory changes.

A blueprint for action on the environment

- a phase-out of the chlorine-based bleaches used by the pulp and paper industries by 1993

- elimination of ozone-damaging chlorofluorocarbons by 1995

- reduction of all discharges of toxic chemicals into air and water to zero by the year 2000

- a halt to the construction of nuclear power plants and eventual phase-out of existing plants

- legislation to eliminate excess packaging and require that all bottles be refillable

- an environmental bill of rights

We feel that educators not directly involved in the environmental movement need to pick up the sense of urgency held by our colleagues working from within. We need to keep in touch with the latest thinking so that we are not, for instance, supporting recycling when we should be talking about reducing the amount produced.

This single-issue focus has successfully reached a broad public but it runs the risk of being co-opted by the dominant agenda. The movement is still primarily middle class, appealing to people's individual concerns, but it has the potential for being linked to deeper economic structural issues and involving broader participation. As educators for social change we all should be interested in linking environmental concerns in our work with a broader race, class, and gender analysis. This will help support those in the environmental movement working to build a critical awareness among front-line environmental activists as they assess, among other issues, the impact of corporate "green campaigns".

Educators and activists together need to urgently deal with the environment versus jobs position that some working-class people take and which companies are eager to promote. Confronting surface contradictions can help us uncover the forces that stand behind them and find common ground for fighting the root causes of these conflicts.

We also need to look at our personal practices as educators, including the amount of paper we use and the kind of marker pens we buy. Can we design a more sane pace into our workshops to get off the treadmill and feel nourished by our interactions? And can we begin to learn from the worldview of First Nations people and work more in harmony with the natural world around us?

185

Humanizing the workplace

The dominant agenda

By all accounts technological change in the 1990s will make previous decades appear stationary.

Communications, computers, and the related high-tech field will concentrate on new hardware – the machines that do things quicker and cheaper. Low-Tech forms of industrial production such as manual assembly work won't disappear but will more and more likely be farmed out to low-wage zones. Dominant interests are likely to continue to feed popular lore that technology is the price of progress and uncontrollable.

Talk about "tech change" can itself be a weapon that management uses to discipline a workforce asking for a greater share of the pie. Linked to tech change is "cultural engineering", which uses training and team-concept initiatives to reorganize work – all part of management initiatives to win hearts and minds.

The popular agenda/implications for educators

Traditionally, working-class response to tech change has been defensive. A few unions, however, have decided to try and tap into the tremendous potential that might result from the creative application of science for the greatest good. For example, the dirtiest jobs that are the greatest risk to workers' health can usefully be done by robots. And the new machinery in the world isn't worth a hill of beans without the corresponding human know-how to run it.

Pro-active union negotiation has resulted in management beginning to recognize the importance of consulting workers about when to shut down a car-assembly line as well as about how to eliminate backbreaking work. Workers in some defence industries in the United States and England have pushed for job security but opposed armaments production. To switch plant production to non-military activities requires labour to go on the offensive and provide a corporate plan to rival that of management: no longer a passive audience in the drama of technological change, labour instead needs to become the primary script-writer.

As educators we have to come to grips with tech change in our own backyard. The FAX machine provides tremendous new opportunities for team planning and design when not all team members live in a common geographic area. In workshops, video technology is often felt to be intrusive but we can harness it to enhance learning opportunities or to provide a graphic record of a session that participants can refer back to.

As we use these tools we have to challenge the concentration of ownership and the control over technological innovation that tends to favour dominant interests. Workers will need support from other sectors, including radical engineers, sociologists, and popular educators. Together these groups can work not only to unmask the dominant agenda and counter the cultural engineering offensive but also to help shape tech change for our benefit.

The humanization of work is about **more** than technological change. To name just a few, it is also about

✧ building respect for worker knowledge
✧ linking skills training to working people's experience and interests
✧ looking at questions of power and hierarchy (especially in countering cultural engineering)
✧ re-valuing the importance of job security amidst rapid changes
✧ asking questions about the size of the workplace in the future.

These are all critical issues as we struggle for a more humane workplace.

DEBORAH BARNDT

CULTURAL AND
IDEOLOGICAL
CHALLENGES

**Democracy: the
threat of a good
example**

The dominant agenda

We looked *democracy* up in the dictionary to find that it comes from the Greek words "demos", or "people", and "kratos", which means "strength". The dictionary says that the people are the rulers in a democracy. Today this proposition is not doing so well in Canada, where central areas of decision-making have been largely excluded from popular participation and public control.

Capitalism's command structure, based on the use of private power often cloaked in secrecy, stands in stark contrast to the more open and horizontal relations of inclusiveness most people equate with democracy. Private power-centres reserve the privilege of decision-making for themselves when it comes to investment, nature, and the conditions of productive work, for instance.

What we are left with is a formal sense of democracy that is often equated in the public's mind with elections. In control of the economy and communications, a small elite of owners and managers also uses the political system to advance its ends. To keep investment decisions safe from social control, business leaders invest in political parties and influence their platforms.

DEBORAH BARNDT

188

The popular agenda/implications for educators

Participatory democracy is the terrain that the popular movement will continue to use for its fight. In Canada the unions, community groups, co-ops, and issue-oriented organizations will continue to play a key role in bringing about needed changes in the 1990s. Broad coalitions such as the Pro-Canada Network are challenging the notion that investment decisions with tremendous social implications are a private sector preserve.

As for elections, the New Democratic Party and some smaller political parties know the importance of keeping corporate funds at arms length if they want to continue representing popular sector interests and to be deserving of their votes. The rank and file of these parties has also discussed reforming the current electoral system with an eye to introducing changes to make it more representational.

As social change educators we need to play our part in returning some of the original lustre to the word "democracy". This change needs to start at the base, in our own organizations, and it needs to be reflected in our daily work as "democratic practice". For this to be more than a slogan, we all need to tackle our own hierarchical organizational structures and help make them more collegial. We also need to shape programs that encourage broad participation and empower people to take the next step in challenging oppressive societal structures.

· As educators we also have a role to play in challenging the narrowing of democracy to mean "elections" and to push for a truly participatory model. The broader public, ourselves included, needs to have a chance to discuss, to disagree, and to agree on how decisions are made. Part of this process is being able to share experiences and perspectives across cultures and continents, which will help us see what has worked, what hasn't, and why.

Democratic processes that work from the base up are a threat to those who currently sit comfortably at the top. One thing these people fear more than anything else is something that works and that they can't control: the threat of a good example.

DEBORAH BARNDT

**Arts and media:
freeing the
imagination**

The dominant agenda

The Canadian elites who helped shape the dominant economic, political, and social agenda in the 1980s have also targeted the cultural agenda for attention. Communication and the arts hold the potential to set our minds free – to not only help us interpret the routines and habits of daily life but also push us to imagine a life beyond the normal bounds. Although the technologies involved may not be in and of themselves politically loaded, ownership or sponsorship can set limits to what is to be communicated and to whom.

From the advertisers who support programs or magazines that help sell their products, to the television producers who shape their work with potential sponsors in mind, we do get an invitation to dream – but it's about their "must have" consumer items. It's a recipe that unintentionally shows up the hollowness of their version of everyday life.

Built as they are around a "star" system, movies, television, and the high-status arts – even newspapers – tend to feature human interest stories rather than stressing the potential power of a wider collectivity. When it is not being exclusive, prime-time television (like Hollywood before it) tends to be divisive by separating "us" off from "them": a subtle but pervasive form of discrimination stands behind a media megamessage linking "bad" with "foreign, dark-skinned, violent, poor" – people out to destroy our good way of life. We are being asked constantly to commit ourselves to a predominately White, powerful, wealthy, and male perspective, no matter what our colour, gender, age, or class background.

Above all, the dominant cultural agenda is effective. Our exclusion from the realm of the stars doesn't mean that most of us don't rush to get autographs – we do. Role models from Hollywood fill our dreams and limit our imagination.

DEBORAH BARNDT

The popular agenda/implications for educators

Community culture has not been eclipsed entirely by commercial culture or the high-status arts, but it has been influenced. The word "amateur" used to be held in high esteem as signifying an involvement without monetary gain or motivation. That concept has come into disrepute with all the emphasis now placed on the professional, who is paid to be the best.

Although skill level is important to improving on craft, grassroots productions are often one of the few ways a community has of expressing itself. Luckily, the participation of familiar people in a production continues to be a drawing card for performances in neighbourhood venues. The concept of artists in residence or the workplace is an attempt to bridge the gap between artist and community. The Popular Theatre Alliance and the increasing number of alternative music and theatre festivals are examples of locally based initiatives with national connections. These networks and events help us recall our unwritten history and also experiment with new forms and content that can feed the inquiring mind.

We have been fortunate to have the publicly funded Canadian Broadcasting Corporation (CBC). Although commercial considerations and severe cutbacks in regional programming have put a brake on CBC Television's potential, it is still a vehicle capable of communicating some wild and occasionally unsettling ideas. Without the CBC and the National Film Board, the art forms of First Nations and newer and poorer Canadians would seldom if ever reach a national audience. Culture has often been the lifeblood of popular sector mobilization. Nowhere has this connection been closer than in the nationalist struggles in Quebec, particularly in the 1960s and 1970s.

As popular educators we know the creativity that can be unleashed through the use of lively participatory activities in our workshops. Once they've tried it themselves, participants become more aware that you don't have to be a professional actor or singer to role-play or compose a song. The activities give us all confidence to look for creative forms in daily life, to revalue grassroots cultural productions and to critically examine the choices we are constantly being led to make.

While we argue that high-status arts, commercial culture, and community culture are not either intrinsically radical or reactionary, ownership and control of arts and culture can make all the difference. And it should be unmasked.

We need to think about expanding connections with dissident elements in the high arts world. And we need to give greater thought both to communications that are effective and inexpensive and to making better use of the established media opportunities. But the task of giving new life, spirit, and force to our education and organizing efforts requires building a deeper understanding of culture – tapping into our histories, memories, identities, and forms of expression both at a collective and an individual level.

As educators, whatever we can do to expand our collective capacities to imagine other possible futures will be key to building a more just, humane, and democratic society.

191

BREAKING
DOWN
BARRIERS,
BUILDING LINKS

As Herbet de Souza, a Brazilian educator, once said, "Social change is more like algebra than arithmetic." We, the authors, certainly think that the twelve challenges we have just put to paper are not to be treated as a matter of "one plus one" or as a formula to be adopted in a linear fashion. On the contrary, we think it's possible that any two of them together could turn out to have the power of ten.

But what we hope we've communicated is our belief that the role of the social change educator is to break down the hegemony of dominant interests and to strengthen the legitimacy of popular groups and their capacity to take on those power structures. When we put these dozen challenges back into a larger picture, we focus once again on the interrelated nature of the oppressions we face. As social change educators we need to work at linking our educational work to organizing, to political action, and to building social movements – in the process forging new relationships from the ground up.

When and where any of these twelve sites of struggle will catch fire, we're not sure. But we are sure that there's a change a-comin' – and we hope to see you there.

DMI ARCHIVES

192

Postscript

Usually we just see the final product of a writing project: the book. We rarely get glimpses into the process of writing it. So that's exactly what this first part of the postscript is about. It's a conversation among ourselves – as five authors – about writing this book collectively:

⋄ starting from what we have in common
⋄ the differences that emerged and what they meant
⋄ the learning – about ourselves, education, and politics.

Using this framework and with most of the writing behind us, we sat down and began to talk. Here are some bits and pieces from that conversation.

About naming

I didn't actually have words for some of the things that I did and saw others do. So part of working on the book was not just about naming power relations, contradictions, or dynamics but had to do with pulling out from our toes ways of describing what we do – the principles we act from. Because often we just do things by our instinct. For me that "pulling out from the toes" is hard labour.

About taking ourselves seriously

Taking ourselves seriously has been a theme as we wrote. So much of what we do is hidden, not valued, that it makes us defensive. The process of the book is about asserting the legitimacy in what we do. It's about all the issues of "naming" that don't come up until you try to speak about your experience. A lot of what's in this book was unspoken before.

About speaking from our own experience

Remember, we began by saying we would simply speak from our experience. But speak about what in our experience? And how would that be useful to someone else?

The writing was a focus for distilling the experience and then naming it from there.

For me, working on this book took my own experience further. I began writing about things I thought I knew about, like the spiral model, and did a first draft. But after you all pulled it apart, I learned a lot more about design from your input. Even the frame of planning, design, and facilitation really emerged from these discussions.

I also realized how much we freeze things into categories – and when you put it down, you realize that the frame isn't quite adequate. Sometimes I didn't know what I was talking about – in "planning", for example. I've been doing this work for all this time, but I didn't really know what the word meant.

193

About reflecting on our practice

I got started on the writing late. I also had this block about "facilitation", and "education for social change". I always thought the context had to be a workshop situation – outside of the formal system. I had seen myself as facilitating learning – not just giving students a recipe but helping them critically analyse. I didn't know if people out there would want to know about that – maybe people would only be interested in the informal settings.

So it was difficult for me to begin. I had done some thinking about myself as a participant researcher – giving voice to people who would not otherwise have voice. Publishing was a way of giving back to people their words so they could use the book as a vehicle for speaking to the wider community. So that's why in my first draft the emphasis was on research. Then I moved from that and started looking at my work generally, to see how much my teaching and other work is littered with political messages or framework: engaging students in conversation rather than "telling them".

The other night I had a dialogue with the students and afterwards I thanked them for the discussion and said I'd learned a lot. Everyone was surprised. "How could you say you learned from us?" they wanted to know. For them, learning is what they do. What I do is inform. So I had to start rethinking and it was good for me. Of course, the pressure of deadlines also helped a lot.

On choosing/writing our own chapters

We chose the chapters that we were each going to write ourselves – not really knowing what we were choosing. So we have no one else to blame. Somehow it worked out and I was glad that I wrote my chapter – or at least that someone else wrote the other chapters and not me.

Once I started to look at my piece (chapter six), I wished it was ten years ago. There was more order then somehow. I knew what the limits were – how the world was divided, the gaps. Suddenly I wondered what was going on. Instead of writing in a time when you know what oppressive structures you're pushing against, now is a time of incredible fluidity. It's hard to know what direction things are taking. It's a new ballgame in many dimensions, especially at the international level. I was also overawed by the assignment of my chapter. So it's been a hard process for me.

On the other hand, I realize I'm not the only one in this boat. No one I've talked to out there has a clear idea of where things are going either. So I semi-relaxed. In all the other chapters we are pulling out from our own experience, flawed as it may be. This chapter is different – we're looking forward.

I felt another pressure too. In doing the type of work I do, I come up against the academics who see popular education/social change educators as "flaky". According to them, we are super-good at keeping people happy and moving them around, but we have no facts, no analysis. So recognizing that while it wouldn't be a definitive statement, this chapter would be important to add to the general agenda, something to kick around.

About writing collectively

One of the interesting things for me is how we've worked. I found myself writing for the four of you. Even though we didn't have a thousand meetings, I was conscious of "how you four would see this, or express that". So it was like having all five people in my head as I was sitting in front of the computer screen. And I think that's how I overcame part of the sense of being overwhelmed.

My assignment was to take the tradition of political economy analysis (which in the left has been structured in a very particular way: solo, detached, and deductive) and bring our own work in as the entry point and go from there. For me, that was like taking on Gramsci directly. In doing that, one resource was the active and implicit involvement of all five people and everyone's thought processes, which are all very different. My thought process is putting out a few ideas, playing with them, and then developing them. At the end you put on a framework.

For example, if you have cider and wine, you think of how to prepare them. Then you look at how they're different and work from there. The weakness of my approach is a tendency to pragmatism and a weak framework. Its strength is that it's tailored to the situation. So, in the process of dialogue, I was forced to formulate things in ways that would make sense to the four of you. I felt if you four understood, the rest of the world would too.

For me, the collective aspect was the most pronounced when I tried to put all the comments together. I'd have all the sheets in front of me and look at what each of you said on a particular page. Maybe I'd begin with one person's page – then chuck that and use someone else's. It's part of working collectively – to speak with someone and sense them speaking back as you try to interpret.

It's amazing that things we find so clear become unclear, because people are having different experiences with the material.

Having to comment on each other's stuff and take it seriously was great. It always had a bearing on something I was trying to think through myself, and not only for this book. But my biggest fear was that I had nothing to say. I start from that fear every time I write and it always takes me a long time to get enough down to tentatively show to people. If they don't burn it, I get the courage to go on. So my fear was to get past the point where the four of you would even consider my draft. Then the fear went and the process was as the rest of you describe.

I experience that same fear. Maybe it has something to do with being a woman?

About voice

I learned a lot about the issue of voice. Some of you pointed out to me the way I used "you" and the corporate "it". I knew about that in theory, especially from feminist literature. But I learned a lot in doing the writing about how I still fall into the traps. In talking about "we" I needed to think about who "we" are. In using "it" I was often disappearing whatever "it" stood for.

Who "we" are is an issue that ran right throughout the book. The process of doing the writing raised questions for me about how often we use "we" to be inclusive and how specifically we were using it here to mean "we five". Then we had to confront who "I" am in the "we".

About being specific

I actually learned something about how you can edit usefully – knowing how much I appreciated when you gave me concrete examples, or spent time reworking something. I didn't know how to do that for other people before.

The importance of being specific comes out here. We are five people who have been talking systematically for four years. A common text forces us to get very specific about what we think: isolate points on which we disagree and find a higher level on which we have consensus.

I think in that sense it's like the ink-blot test. It serves as a way of locating ourselves and our trajectories in relation to each other as well as to the rest of the world. In terms of my own work, the writing is a part of the rest of my life. So I find myself explaining the spiral model to a colleague in the union. I never had words or an image to explain to him before.

About having fun writing

I remember those days when we were high, joyful – when we had moved to another point on something. I've had wonderful moments in this process. I'd bring a draft without knowing how to move forward, get input. Then, saying "wow", I'd go back to the computer. It's the first time I've ever had good times writing – moments where I felt really good.

I got inspired. I would read some parts and there would be flashes of brilliance. None of us has the whole thing, but suddenly as I read I'd say, "That's fantastic – brilliant – where did that come from?" In that sense there is a dynamic which is packaged as competitive which, in a context like this, is synergy.

I can't resist this story. I was reading my draft with comments from one of you where you came to a place of "brilliance" and wrote "YES!" on the page. I howled with laughter since it was a paragraph I had lifted from that same person's input on an earlier draft, which I had thought was a moment of brilliance.

About humility

I like the spirit that runs through the book. I believe that we have some extremely important resources in the DMI and its network for pushing the popular agenda forward in this country at this moment. On the other hand, I like that the book is humble, that it doesn't say this is the recipe we've been cooking up for three years and now it's baked. I like that spirit and would be surprised if we don't get comments about that – that it's good to state our limitations as we write.

For me personally it's been a process of running up against the limits of what we can possibly know. When I haven't included suggested changes in a rewrite, it's been because I didn't know how to do it.

On looking into the future

We left out a lot of important issues in chapter six – like youth, ability/disability, the situation facing farmers and fishermen.

One of the strengths of that chapter is that the connections are alluded to but it's not all tied up. It's not as if we, the enlightened vanguard, have sorted it all out. So here are the primary and secondary contradictions – and here's what you need to do. This has been the traditional political discourse we've rejected but we haven't always come up with an alternative discourse.

An invitation

I think that the tone of the book is one of invitation – inviting people to experiment with design, adapt tools, and put their own educated guesses forward for criticism and shaping. I think that tone of invitation can help social movements to grow. We are not about maintaining progressive groups and organizations as private clubs.

I think the question of language can be situated in the context of invitation. In a lot of the work I do, the question of language comes up in people's unease in using any words to name things for fear they'll be wrong. This invitation is to try out words to see if they describe or name, as best one can, what's going on right now.

About language

For me the question of language is saying, "That term doesn't work – so I'll try this one." You then leave it in the cupboard because there are some other things to go on to. This writing has required me to take the stuff and dust it off and look at whether I need new terms.

I was doing that all the time in my chapter. Do we use Black people, people of colour? Whatever we decide, whose words and meanings are those?

Words also change with time. At another time, in relating to issues around Native people, we were clear they wanted to be called "Native people", not "Indians". Now "First Nations" is important because politically it's a different moment. And "First Nations" is a political statement. So it matters very much how people refer to themselves. We need to say, "This is the best we know now." If we were writing a year from now, we might be using different words.

READERS
RESPOND:
SOME QUOTES

The readers of the draft manuscript had a very short time to do a lot of work – and they all came through for us. We have incorporated many of their comments and suggestions into the text itself. But they also made general comments that raised new questions for us, and we want to share those comments with you here. In keeping with the rest of the book, we have not attached specific names to the quotes. The names of all of the readers are noted in the acknowledgements.

On taking care of ourselves

How about a really strong piece on the importance of not packing the agenda? For example, Fran Endicott has a principle: one activity per block of time. The underlying principles for me being:

1 we can't do everything, so what's most important to do?
2 if we keep the breadth from getting away from us, maybe we can have some depth.
3 we want to learn/practice resistance to the culture of burn-out, which is essentially a weapon against ourselves.

Audre Lorde in *Burst of Light* (her cancer journals) says, "Caring for myself is not self-indulgence, it is self-preservation, and that is an art of political warfare."

I think the value of popular education as a creative tool is a very important point – what helps us laugh together, to create and re-shape our world together. The task of nurturing ourselves and each other is something we tend to forget – we burn ourselves out – we lose our ability to laugh. The spiritual *can* be political.

On the tone of the book

Another comment about tone. At one point I commented on what I said was an excessively "apologetic" tone.... I don't think you need to be defensive or to seem to be defensive. There's a tension between arrogance and humility. There's a fine line between criticism (especially self-criticism) and apology. There is a kind of personal defensiveness which no doubt relates to the interpersonal context of the kind of work you all have committed your lives to. This is a reality that I have felt myself all too often – and never really figured out how to resolve for myself.

Actually, much of the value of your manuscript is in giving me personal insight about these very same feelings in myself, about what to do differently.

On the differences in voices, styles

I liked not knowing who wrote what. It gave me a collective sense of the basis of what I was reading. (And it was fun to guess).

I loved the many voices – like a Latin American novel.

I like the voice shifts as a model for diversity.

For me the mixed voices in one volume mostly does not work.

198

On power   Because our struggle against hierarchical arrangement of power is constant, I think we have become in regard to "power" something like the flip side of the liberal educators who recognize difference but not inequity. The challenge is to understand the uses of power and the choices we have available for the employment of power.

"Respect the people you teach. Empower people through learning." These are both liberal platitudes which do not "respect" people. I think it should be stated – perhaps more succinctly – that these expressions easily serve to reinforce lopsided power relations, neopower relations. When we talk about "teaching people" or "empowering them", a position of power is assumed by the teacher – as the one doing both the "teaching" and the "empowering".

My sense is that it all goes back to the power of language. In this case, the language is used to protect our territory, our control, our sphere of influence, while seeming to mouth change. It makes it possible to talk about democracy and democratic practice without giving up power.

On activities for seeking new information   It would be useful to have a tip or two about the process of seeking information beyond the workshop. What I mean is: the presumption of all or nearly all the activities seems to be that all the information and insight the participants will need to accomplish what they want, already exists within the group. And yet one major problem activists need to solve is how to gather "information" that will help them in their struggles.

Information gathering in this sense might involve:

◇ identifying general topics of active concern and relevance, specific questions whose answers would be helpful in addressing those general topics of concern
◇ identifying possible sources of information (in the group, local organizations, and beyond)
◇ clarifying good ways to access this information
◇ clarifying ways to figure out what the gathered information "says" that might be useful for action-strategies.

I don't mean to retreat to the reification of "experts" and "expert knowledge". In fact, that's part of the challenge here: maintaining participants' respect for the power of their own expertise and insight, while at the same time supporting their ability (individually and collectively) to seek and find the kinds of information they will need to help accomplish what they want to accomplish.

About language

I was struck with your comments in the postscript about the use of "we" because that is something I wanted to write to you about too. Sometimes I felt a bit put-off by what seemed to me your ambiguous use of "we". Sometimes you very clearly meant you five.... Other times you seemed to mean we-educators-for-social-change ... a more inclusive use of "we". So this latter use of "we" includes me. But sometimes the usages went back and forth – in a way that I sometimes felt roped me into your assertions, your knowledge, without my consent. I felt a bit patronized. Your honesty throughout the manuscript helped me get beyond my own personal defensiveness.

Surprisingly, what I really didn't like was your introduction ... I had problems with the non-user friendliness of the language. For example: The craft of democratic practice is judging the timing and content of what we say, so that we move people forward, rather than indulging in our own need to be heard. When I read this sentence I asked myself: "What is the craft of democratic practice? Democracy as espoused by the American/Canadian state?

Judging and timing and content of what we say. Well, politicians in this so-called democratic practice of governing in Canada really judge their timing and content to fit the audience in the most offensive and manipulative way. Is this what is meant by this statement?

So that we move people forward. This sounded anti-participatory, almost like forcing people to go forward when they might want to go clockwise, or bounce thoughts around like billiard balls, so what is the direction "forward" and in whose eyes is a direction forward and not backward or sideways?

Indulging in our own need to be heard. Does this mean a popular educator has no voice? But just facilitates others? It certainly is a thought-provoking sentence; but it didn't give me any assurance that my questions would be answered in future chapters.

I started to mount an argument in my mind.... Where were you all coming from and had you become conservative in the last couple of years????!! It was a great relief to find everything falling into place as I read the other chapters.

About the people we work with

Is transformational education only with oppressed people? Can a person who does not come from an oppressed class be an effective facilitator with their oppressed brothers and sisters? What gives that person the right to be a facilitator for someone else's change process? How can we ensure that the facilitator doesn't "take over" the change process? The answers are alluded to in other chapters where you stress the importance of facilitators locating ourselves as actors, identifying our own social and organizational identity.

Can we say that we are engaged in transformational education if, for example, we are working with an all-White, fairly wealthy, middle-aged group of church goers ... people who could not class themselves as oppressed? Some may even see themselves as oppressors but who want to change?

On ownership of the event by participants

Ownership of the event by the majority of participants ... means that the event is "messy", the agenda is continually being changed by the participant-dominated steering committee, whole planned sections will have had to be reworked or dumped in order to meet the participants' needs, participants become agitated by the framework and the agenda and start to challenge the planners, and I face each major session with great trepidation, until the middle of the event, the participants take over, they own the event and they pull it off!

I see my role as setting the stage to ensure that the conditions are ripe for the participants to take over. If an event isn't messy, and people don't start challenging me, then I start to worry. I know that something is terribly wrong.

Control: it seems to me that an integral part of the spiral approach is control, as sense of ownership of the process. I would find it useful if this was consciously and deliberately named as one of the stages in a workshop. This is not to suggest that there's a beginning-and-end model but a time when this is placed on the table.

On making the context visible

Making context visible and talkable is an important issue which might be more explicitly discussed. Context is a key characteristic of education for the nineties as links to environment (constructed and natural) and attempts to draw attention to the importance of a sense of place – metaphorically and materially speaking.

Challenges to transformational educational work

In the public mind, the experience and model of source countries – Cuba and Nicaragua, etc. – for transformational educational work are now profoundly questioned and, in several vital dimensions, discredited. We therefore ask: What does it say for the role of this educational practice? There? Here? This book twice alludes to this issue. It is a very partial response to a question which threatens to make this education even more marginal in the eyes of many.

What's missing

The importance and role of culture – its deeper meaning, how it gets recovered, expressed, integrated into educating and organizing for change.

The real challenge and complexity of linking our educational work to organizing, to political action, to movement-building.

Outsider-insider

Most pieces appear based on the practice of facilitators as outsiders working with an organization or group for a limited period of time. This outsider-insider dynamic, and the differences of the experiences of facilitators in those two positions might be useful to name and address more explicitly; also to include more examples from those who do work within organizations, because it is a different experience and I think it reflects the majority of the readers.

On endings I like the idea that you will including a section that "reveals" your work – thereby demystifying the process. However, I think that it is rather long, and a bit hard to follow.... Whatever [you do with it], the Postscript as it stands now is definitely not a good way to end the book.

You who think I find words for everything
this is enough for now
cut it short   cut loose from my words

You for whom I write this
in the night hours when the wrecked cartilage
sifts round the mystical jointure of the bones
when the insect of detritus crawls
from shoulder to elbow to wristbone
remember: the body's pain and the pain on the streets
are not the same   but you can learn
from the edges that blur   O you who love clear edges
more than anything   watch the edges that blur

Adrienne Rich
from *Your Native Land, Your Life: Poems*

Bibliography

To help us decide what to include in this bibliography we used the following guidelines:

◇ more on practice than theory
◇ must be in print and available
◇ major works of DMI members
◇ only books, kits, booklets – no articles.

Materials distributed by the Doris Marshall Institute are coded "★".

1. THE PRACTICE OF EDUCATION FOR SOCIAL CHANGE

★ Arnold, Rick, Deborah Barndt, and Bev Burke. *A New Weave: Popular Education in Canada and Central America.* Toronto: CUSO and OISE, 1985. *A New Weave* selects four new ideas or designs from the Central American experience and reworks them for an advanced industrial context.

★ Arnold, Rick and Bev Burke. *A Popular Education Handbook.* Toronto: CUSO and OISE, 1983. Based on over forty workshops, the book has practical examples of applying a popular education approach to Central American solidarity education.

★ Barndt, Deborah. *Naming the Moment: Political Analysis for Action: A Manual for Community Groups.* Toronto: The Jesuit Centre, 1989. An introduction to the four-phase approach to political analysis that is called "naming the moment". It includes examples of how groups have used this approach to analyse their own issues.

Barndt, Deborah. *To Change This House: Popular Education in Nicaragua.* Toronto: Between the Lines, 1991. A study of how the Sandinistas introduced popular education to Nicaragua in the 1980s. Includes many photographs.

Barndt, Deborah, Ferne Cristall, and dian marino. *Getting There: Producing Photostories with Immigrant Women.* Toronto: Between the Lines, 1982. An introduction to a collective method of learning based on personal and social experience. Also includes provocative photoessays.

Boal, Agusto. *Theatre of the Oppressed.* London: Pluto Books, 1979.

Cristall, Ferne and Barbara Emanuel. *Images in Action: A Guide to Using Women's Film and Video.* Toronto: Between the Lines, 1986. Simple, easy-to-follow advice on the use of films and videos in education programs. Includes a section on feminist filmmaking.

CUSO Development Education. *Basics and Tools: A Collection of Popular Education Resources and Activities.* Ottawa: CUSO, 1985. A handbook of basic models and principles of experiential adult learning, as well as a compilation of popular education exercises, role plays, simulation games, and activities for development education.

Czerny, Michael S.J., and Jamie Swift. *Getting Started on Social Analysis in Canada.* Second edition. Toronto: Between the Lines, 1988. Offers approaches and techniques for people wanting to develop skills for understanding social issues or for helping others to develop those skills.

Cunningham, Frank, Sue Findlay, Marlene Kadar, Alan Lennon, and Ed Silva. *Social Movements Social Change: The Politics and Practice of Organizing.* Toronto: Between the Lines, 1988.

Doris Marshall Institute. *Educating for a Change: Workshop Manual Series.* DMI: Toronto, 1989-90. These four manuals document DMI skillshops on facilitation and design with the African National Congress, Education Wife Assault, Immigrant Service Organizations, and the Ontario Public Service Employees Union.

GATT-Fly. *Ah-Hah! A New Approach to Popular Education.* Toronto: Between the Lines, 1983. Illustrates the Ah-Hah! seminar technique of drawing to illustrate connections between the lives of participants and broader economic and social structures.

Hammond, Merryl and Rob Collins. *Self-Directed Learning: Critical Practice.* London: Kogan Page, 1991. Based on the experience of the authors in health education in South Africa.

Hope, Anne, Sally Timmel, and Chris Hodzi. *Training for Transformation: A Handbook for Community Workers.* Three volumes. Zimbabwe: Mambo Press (P.O. Box 66002, Kopje, Harare, Zimbabwe), 1984. This book is written for community educators and is based on twelve years of experience with groups in Africa. Part one is on the theory of Paulo Freire; part two focuses on the skills necessary for participatory education; and part three looks at social analysis.

James, Carl. *Making It: Black Youth, Racism and Career Aspirations in a Big City.* Oakville, Ont.: Mosaic Press, 1990. Black youth in Toronto talk with the author about their world: about dealing with racism, about their aspirations.

★ James, Carl. *Seeing Ourselves: Exploring Race, Ethnicity and Culture.* Toronto: Sheridan College, 1989. Canadian college students of different backgrounds write about their identity and reflect on the socialization processes that have influenced their ideas and attitudes. Contextualized by the author with examples of racism, prejudice, stereotyping, discrimination, and ethnocentrism.

Kokopeli, Bruce and George Lakey. *Leadership for Change: Towards a Feminist Model.* Philadelphia: New Society Publishers, 1978. This booklet looks at the functions of leaders and how to use feminist perspectives of shared leadership to break away from authoritarian patriarchal styles.

Lee, Enid. *Letters to Marcia: A Teacher's Guide to Anti-Racist Education.* Toronto: Cross Cultural Communications Centre, 1985. Through letters to a teacher named Marcia, Enid Lee shares her concerns and outlines some practical activities to assist Canadian educators in furthering anti-racist education.

Maclean, Eleanor. *Between the Lines: How to Detect Bias and Propaganda in the News and Everyday Life.* Montreal: Black Rose Books, 1981. This book teaches us to "read between the lines", offering activities, exercises, and research suggestions. Some data needs updating (such as ownership of the media in Canada), but it's still a useful tool.

Maguire, Patricia. *Doing Participatory Research.* Amherst, Mass.: Center for International Education, School of Education, University of Massachusetts, 1987.

Marshall, Doris. *Silver Threads: Critical Reflections on Growing Old.* Toronto: Between the Lines, 1987. Doris Marshall recounts her own story and in the process challenges the negative images of ageing that are so dominant today.

★ Marshall, Judith, with Domingos Chigarire, Helena Francisco, Antonio Goncalves, and Leonardo Nhantumbo. *Training for Empowerment: A Kit of Materials based on an Exchange among Literacy Workers in Mozambique, Brazil and Nicaragua.* Toronto: International Council for Adult Education (ICAE) and DMI, 1990. This kit grew out of a South-South exchange program that took four Mozambican literacy workers to Latin America. The kit highlights experiences and approaches to training encountered along the way and represents them in a hands-on manner useful to grassroots educators.

Mukherjee, Alok, Tim McCaskell, and Hari Lalla. *Did you hear the one about...? Dealing with Racist Jokes.* Toronto: Learnxs Press, 1987. (Available through the Toronto Board of Education.) Using cartoons and text, this booklet analyses racist jokes and suggests ways of responding to them.

Progressive Literacy Group. *Writing on Our Side.* Vancouver: Progressive Literacy Group, 1986. While the starting point for this useful booklet is that people should express themselves clearly, it goes beyond "plain English" and gives practical tips for detecting the "corporate English" bias in our style of writing.

Thomas, Barb and Charles Novogrodsky. *Combatting Racism in the Workplace: A Course for Workers.* Toronto: Cross Cultural Communications Centre, 1983. This book outlines ten sessions designed to help workers learn about and work together against racism. A complementary set of readings was developed to use in the course.

Thomas, Barb. *Multiculturalism at Work: A Guide to Organizational Change.* Toronto: YWCA, 1987. Although this book is about organizational change, it has useful reference material on anti-racist training.

Women's Self-Help Network. *Women's Self-Help Educational Kit.* Courtenay, B.C.: Ptarmigan Press, 1984. This three-volume resource is grounded in a participatory approach to the training of peer group counsellors and includes many concrete examples of activities.

2. THE THEORY AND METHODOLOGY OF EDUCATION FOR SOCIAL CHANGE

Brookfield, Stephen D. *Developing Critical Thinkers: Challenging Adults to Explore Alternative Ways of Thinking and Action.* Keynes England: Open University Press, 1987.

Brookfield, Stephen D. *Understanding and Facilitating Adult Learning.* San Francisco: Jossey-Bass, 1988.

Bunch, Charlotte and Sandra Pollack. *Learning Our Way: Essays in Feminist Education.* New York: The Crossing Press, 1983.

Freire, Paulo. *Pedagogy of the Oppressed.* New York: Continuum, 1983.

Freire, Paulo and Ira Shor. *A Pedagogy for Liberation: Dialogues on Transforming Education.* South Hadley, Mass.: Bergin and Garvey, 1986.

Giroux, Henry A. *Theory and Resistance in Education: A Pedagogy for the Opposition.* South Hadley, Mass.: Bergin and Garvey, 1983.

Gramsci, Antonio. *Selections from the Prison Notebooks.* Quintin Hoare and G. Nowell-Smith, editors. New York: International Publications, 1971.

hooks, bell. *Talking Back: Thinking Feminist, Thinking Black.* Toronto: Between the Lines, 1989.

hooks, bell. *Yearning: Race, Gender and Cultural Politics.* Toronto: Between the Lines, 1990.

Lerner, Michael. *Surplus Powerlessness.* Oakland: Institute for Labor and Mental Health, 1986.

Mackie, Robert (ed.). *Literacy and Revolution: The Pedagogy of Paulo Freire.* London: Pluto Press, 1980.

Reed, David. *Education for Building a People's Movement.* Boston: South End Press, 1981.

Searle, Chris. *Words Unchained: Language and Revolution in Grenada.* London: Zed Press, 1984.

Segal, Lynn. *Is the Future Feminine?* London: Virago, 1987.

Shor, Ira. *Critical Teaching and Everyday Life.* Montreal: Black Rose Books, 1980.

Simon, Roger. *Gramsci's Political Thought.* London: Lawrence Wishart, 1982.

Walters, Shirley. *Education for Democratic Participation.* Belville, South Africa: Centre for Adult and Continuing Education (CACE), University of Western Cape, 1989.

Willis, Paul. *Learning to Labour: How Working Class Kids Get Working Class Jobs.* London: Saxon House, 1977.

EDUCATING FOR A CHANGE